Seriously God?

I'm Doing Everything I Know To Do And It's Not Working

Jenny Smith

WestBow
PRESS
A DIVISION OF THOMAS NELSON

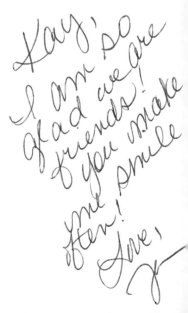

Kay,
I am so
glad we are
friends!
you make
me smile
often!
Love,
J

WestBow Press books may be ordered through booksellers or by contacting:

WestBow Press
A Division of Thomas Nelson
1663 Liberty Drive
Bloomington, IN 47403
www.westbowpress.com
1-(866) 928-1240

ISBN: 978-1-4497-4026-9 (sc)
ISBN: 978-1-4497-4025-2 (e)

Library of Congress Control Number: 2012902530

Printed in the United States of America

WestBow Press rev. date: 2/17/2012

To North Pointe Church.

I've never been to a church like ours. Just like many of you I showed up at North Pointe hurt and disillusioned. You, reached out and not only accepted me, you have loved on me and my family in ways I never could have imagined. Jesus shows brightly in your faces. It is a honor to serve side by side with you.

I pray Jesus gets brighter and brighter in each of us!

Contents

Foreword

As you read *"Seriously God?"* you will be invited into several personal encounters and conversations that Jenny has with God. Come walk with Jenny around her garden as she pours out her heart and frustrations to God and finds out he is big enough to handle them. Then spend time with God and her at the kitchen sink. You'll laugh and cry as she hikes through the woods with her friends and God. Jenny teaches you and me that when we invite and include God in our common, walking—around lives that our lives can become uncommon. Come; discover with Jenny how the great "I Am" is concerned with whatever is concerning you!

Jim Pinkard
Pastor North Pointe Church

Acknowledgments

To Chad: Thank you, for letting me share our struggles in such a public way. You have always been my greatest encourager. I'm so glad you were willing to take a chance the day you said, 'I do'.

To Meghan, Katie and Lauren: You three make me so proud. I love seeing the women you are growing into. Thank you for all your help, all your patience, and all the times you have hung out at church while I taught a class.

To Mom: I love you! Thank you for always helping with the girls, and always being willing to defend me. Makes me smile every time it happens! I have watched you reach out to people and make them smile more times than I can count. You have a gift for making people feel special. I'm proud to call you mom! Tell Dad he's the best grandpa I could imagine for the girls. He spoils them and they love it!

To Geneva: You raised a wonderful son, and I'm very blessed to have you for a mother-in-law. There has never been a time we have asked you for help that you haven't been there for us. Thank you for teaching me so many things; you have made me a better wife and mother.

To Carrie and Laura: You two balance me out! Carrie, you have taught me to serve in ways I would have never done. You inspire me with all you do. There is no one I respect more than you. Laura, your generosity with your talents has been an answer to my prayers. I'm so glad all those years ago you had a desire to share those gifts. I just hope you don't regret your prayer, bet you didn't know in addition to helping someone, you'd be getting a friend, whether you wanted me or not!

To Connie, Becky, Angie, Linda, and Gloria: This book would not be what it is without all your encouragement. You five brings lots of smiles and laughter to my days! Each of you, bring something unique to my life. Thank you for your friendship. More than that, thank you for extending grace to me on several occasions!

To my friends at the food pantry: I'm crazy about you guys! I love how we all come together to serve and leave week after week better for it. Your commitment inspires me in ways I don't think you can even imagine.

To Stacey, Amy, and Amanda: Stacey, you were my first editor! I would dare say, you had to work the hardest. All those days, all your encouragement, all your expertise, makes you a very important part of every word I ever write. Amy, you came along giving of your time and energy, even though we have never met face to face. Amanda, this is our first undertaking together, you have made the words I wrote better! Thank you to each of you for your patience and words of wisdom!

To my critique group, especially Jen: Each of you brought a new dimension to my writing. I love how we all are from such a variety of backgrounds, but we have one common thread, Jesus!

To my Bible study friends: You will never know how God uses you in my life! You encourage me, you challenge my thinking, and you make me laugh out loud some days! I can't wait until we study this together. Nothing makes me happier than opening up the Scriptures with you. You are greatly loved.

To Ed: There aren't many people you can send an email for help and feel confident in not only them doing it, but doing it well. You have done both! Thank you for your friendship all these years, and your support, both mean the world to me. You and Chad make me think and plan, and I'm better for it.

To my Jesus: Thank you for rescuing me. Your word is life to me. It has changed my heart once again. I pray I have shared our journey in a way that brings glory to you, and you only.

Introduction

As I sit looking over my backyard, I realize my arms are feeble and my knees are weak. Life is hard. May I be honest? Hard, I can deal with, but lately life feels like a roller coaster ride I didn't want to get on—and I hate roller coasters. I hate feeling out of control. A large part of my thirty-eight years have been spent knowing I wasn't in control; God is. Regardless of this, I've managed to feel as though a large portion of life *was* in my control to a large degree. Not anymore.

In times past, many of us living right here in the United States experienced an abundant existence. If we wanted a job, we had a job. Gas was cheap, and we drove many a mile for pleasure. Our grocery budgets were set and followed. We had to discipline ourselves, sure, but at the end of the night, for most of us, life made sense. Maybe your family was like mine. When we needed more, my husband, Chad, might take on some extra work. I might use a few more coupons, but all in all, the money needs balanced out.

Not anymore—at least not where I'm sitting, looking over my garden. Now jobs are scarce, gas prices change daily, and groceries are skyrocketing. The general feeling for many of us is a little bit of disbelief mixed with a little fear and a side of, "What's next?"

I spend many mornings desperately seeking God through his Word, and he has faithfully met me there. Recently, though, I felt like something was missing, some kind of depth I couldn't seem to reach. I saw that *something* in other people. I even went to see some of them and tried to put my finger on what I was missing, to no avail. I was doing the same things they were: church, Bible study, prayer, friendships, service—you get the drift. But I couldn't quite put into words what I felt was missing.

We planted our garden to take some of the pressure off of the grocery bill. I thought I would do some canning. We would eat what grew and maybe save a little money. A rabbit came and ate every plant we set out. Not to be discouraged, we put a net fence around the garden to keep the rabbits out; we replanted. The rabbit came back and had another feast!

I bought rabbit and deer repellant, the worst-smelling substance I have ever encountered! Really, I can't even describe how bad it smells. I sprayed every inch around the garden, gagging here and there as I went.

Chad and I stood in the garden in shock. Would you believe those rabbits were still nibbling? Looking around, I thought, *Seriously, God, we are doing everything we know to do, and it's not working!*

The failed garden was the point where all my feelings came to a head and spilled out everywhere. This past year has been filled with more tears than I can count. It's been a year when it seemed as though everyday life was harder and harder, more and more out of control.

While I was riding this roller coaster called life, God wasn't absent. I know he has a plan and a purpose that is good. How can what my heart knows make it to my daily life? That is what's missing. Maybe your situation is different but you know something is just missing. There is some depth you can't seem to find no matter how many Bible studies you attend and no matter what prayer method you try. At the end of the day, if you are completely honest, something just isn't lining up.

I started noticing the phrase "in the name of Jesus." It seemed as though every time I opened my Bible, that wording or one close to it popped off the page. What did those words mean? We close our prayers with "in the name of Jesus." I could even tell you the phrase relates to the authority we now have in Christ. But do I really understand *what* "in the name of Jesus" means?

I taught a lesson out of Exodus where I read "since my Name is in him" (Exodus 23:21 NIV), and I realized God was trying to get my attention. I looked up every verse with that phrasing and started connecting some dots. The people of the early church knew and operated their daily lives out of the power of the name of Jesus. Do I? Do you?

Just like us, the people of the early church were on a roller coaster that jerked them around and pushed them to dizzying heights, only to plunge them to the depths, over and over. That's what this journey is about—a search for some depth of relationship with God, a depth of relationship others can see in the way we live. It is a depth that, even as we stand smack dab in the middle of life, causes our arms to be strong and knees steadfast, regardless of daily changes. I needed it to be so.

Do you?

How to use this book

Before each chapter I'll be sharing a question to start you on your journey. After each chapter you'll also find a couple of questions to ponder. Maybe talk with your friends and see what they think. Small groups are a great way to share life with people who can encourage and challenge us in our walk. I hope some of you are doing this book with your small groups. The questions at the end of the chapter will make for some interesting conversations. Included also is a status quo challenge, I love a good healthy challenge, don't you?

I'm so thrilled you have decided to join me on this journey. I would love to hear from you, I want to hear your story of the journey you take. I'm praying for you to have a mighty encounter with God! All my contact information is in the back of the book.

Ready, this first question requires you to do just what I did in the garden, get honest about what you're feeling!

Before you start reading this book, please take a moment and briefly list out your top needs.

I Am the Bread of Life

I walked through the house one last time. I knew I had to pull myself together quickly. I paused, looking in the girls' bedrooms, painted exactly how they had wanted. I walked through the living room smiling, remembering when my friend had spent days painting those walls with me. The front door beckoned me to open it one last time. As my hand grasped the knob, all of a sudden, I couldn't do it. I couldn't open that door and walk to the truck piled high with our belongings. My head rested on the frame as tears filled my eyes. How did we get to this place?

Oh, I remembered all the mistakes we had made, but when we finally began to wake up, we immediately turned to God. We had thought he would come through.

He didn't.

Our house was going into foreclosure, we were moving into a rental house, and God didn't seem to care. There was no time to rehash this again; Chad and the girls were waiting. They needed me to put on a smile. It could have been worse. As I walked down those steps, I didn't know it was about to get much worse.

Over the course of two years, like so many families, we faced foreclosure, job loss, the anxiety of no health insurance, and having to learn to adapt to a different income bracket. Somehow, adapting to a higher one had never been an issue.

I struggled with how God had let me down. Where was he? Why didn't he provide a job where we could maintain our standard of living? My whole Christian life had been built on an understanding of God being our provider—the one whom we went to when we had a need. What happened? We were doing everything we knew to do, and it wasn't working.

As I stood in our garden months later, I realized that if I didn't turn to God's Word, I was never going to understand why my reality wasn't lining up with my view of God. I began searching in the book of John and discovered the seven "I am" statements of Jesus. Don't feel bad if you don't know them—neither did I. But as I studied them, my thinking completely changed, causing my heart to undergo a transformation as well.

I'm praying God will do the same mighty work in your heart. That's really what it comes down to—our hearts. We can find plenty of resources to help with some of the practical needs, but our hearts may have been left empty.

As I started considering the phrase "in the name of Jesus," my mind started reciting all his other names: Deliverer, Savior, Emmanuel, Lamb of God, Son of God, Son of Man, and others. While every one of these names is true and worthy of our consideration, in the book of John, we find seven distinct times that Jesus said, "I am . . ." Seven times, we are personally invited to see more clearly who Jesus is. If we are going to live life in the name of Jesus, we need to have a firm grip on who he claims to be. Each time Jesus uses this particular wording—"I am"—in the Greek,[1] it is significant—a solemn pronouncement that only occurs in the book of John. Each "I am" statement highlights a particular relationship of Jesus to the spiritual needs of people, all with the intention of radically getting our undivided attention.

As we start our journey, we find that the Galilean society was an agrarian peasant society. If the Galileans didn't grow or catch their food, they probably didn't eat. On top of having to grow their own food, they also had to pay hefty taxes. Many times, they would lose what little land they had as the result of a bad harvest and burdensome taxes.

More than likely, this group of people did what was expected of them: taking care of their families, going to synagogue, and praying, much as we do. We may be doing the right things, but something is missing. I feel certain they felt something was missing in their daily lives, too, because of what we find them doing—seeking out Jesus. They came to Jesus, because they saw the miracles Jesus performed on the sick. They saw healings and wanted to know more, so they followed him. As they (men, women, and children) walked toward him, what do you think they were thinking?

Jesus' followers were people who lived a very hand-to-mouth existence, struggling to put food on the table, struggling to pay for doctors, and struggling to know that God cared for them. While watering the plants in my garden this morning, I contemplated all the people in times past—and even now—who lived a hand-to-mouth existence. Trust me, my family and I have felt like we were close at times! While I felt desperate as I surveyed the damage from rabbits, I knew in reality that I wouldn't go completely hungry; others aren't that fortunate. What might it be like to really be that desperate? The people we are going to visit in the book of John would have been in those kinds of situations, with very little food—or some days, none. They needed doctors but had to walk to where one was and pray he would treat them, even with no money.

When the poor walked up to Jesus, they were in search of the miraculous! Just like the women who walked that dirt path in Galilee, I walk in search of the one who can do the miraculous. My head knows it. Even my heart knows it. But as I walk this path today, what Jesus is about to say to me—to us—is the same thing he told the Galileans. He gives the same invitation to a life that defies the status quo.

As we start our journey in John 6, we see Jesus at the height of his popularity. Up until this point, Jesus had been gaining in popularity, but as he pulled the curtain back on the deeper aspects of who he is, many walked away. In fact, many of the people who had been following him said, "This is a hard saying; who can listen to it?" (John 6:60). Many got up, dusted themselves off, and walked away, disappointed.

The ones who stayed were transformed into women and men who really knew Jesus—not just in the miraculous moments, but also in the hard truths of life. They were people whom we'll study later in the book of Acts. They lived out these truths even on the roller coaster that defined their lives. They were men and women whose depth of relationship with Christ caused them to flourish—and others as well.

It's kind of scary to realize as we start our study that many of Jesus' followers turned around and went back to the routine of life. The daunting part to me is that these words we are about to examine are left in our hands. Will we change or stay in the status quo? Exactly what truths does Jesus have to reveal to us that have the power to either cause us to turn back or to be like Peter and say, "Lord, to whom shall we go? You have the words of eternal life"? (John 6:68)

Peter agrees that the truth Jesus shared is hard, but where else was he going to go? Maybe he was like some of us who have tried many different ways to be satisfied, with disastrous results. We have now reached the point in our lives where we say, "I'm in. Jesus, you are it."

As you read these verses, picture yourself in the crowd, walking toward Jesus.

> After this Jesus went away to the other side of the Sea of Galilee, which is the Sea of Tiberias. And a large crowd was following him, because they saw the signs that he was doing on the sick. Jesus went up on the mountain, and there he sat down with his disciples. Now the Passover, the feast of the Jews, was at hand. Lifting up his eyes, then, and seeing that a large crowd was coming toward him, Jesus said to Philip, "Where are we to buy bread, so that these people may eat?" He said this to test him, for he himself knew what he would do. Philip answered him, "Two hundred denarii would not buy enough bread for each of them to get a little." (John 6:1-7)

The seven "I am" statements of Jesus are about to be conveyed to us starting during the time of the yearly Passover feast. Each "I am" statement was revealed in a short period of time—one year, to be precise. There was one year from the first "I am" to the last "I am" as Jesus approached his death on the cross of Calvary. Jesus looked at these people and knew it was time to reveal even more of who he is! The first of the "I am" statements was revealed to people who were approaching Jesus because of his ability to heal.

As Jesus looked out over the crowd, his first thought was to supply them with bread—a very basic need. Defining what exactly basic needs are for us can be difficult because of all the resources we have been given. Do we think that since we live in the United States, we get to have more advanced basic needs? Our very real human side might feel that way. However, if we strip all of life down to the commonalities, our basic needs end up being water, food, shelter, clothing, and love. I really don't know what to think of that. I prefer to think of my wants as basic needs, especially when I feel my wants are not extravagant, so they must be basic needs. Could we live without the Internet, cell phones, and the like that make up what we consider necessary for life?

As you read the rest of the story about Jesus feeding the people, don't lose sight of the little boy who offered his five barley loaves and two fish. In Jesus' day, barley loaves were eaten by poor people. Notice what Jesus used when he fed the people.

> One of his disciples, Andrew, Simon Peter's brother, said to him, "There is a boy here who has five barley loaves and two fish, but what are they for so many?" Jesus said, "Have the people sit down." Now there was much grass in the place. So the men sat down, about five thousand in number. Jesus then took the loaves, and when he had given thanks, he distributed them to those who were seated. So also the fish, as much as they wanted. And when they had eaten their fill, he told his disciples, "Gather up the leftover fragments, that nothing may be lost." So they

gathered them up and filled twelve baskets with fragments from the five barley loaves left by those who had eaten. When the people saw the sign that he had done, they said, "This is indeed the Prophet who is to come into the world!" (John 6:8-14)

Jesus met the Galileans' basic need for food, but he fed them barley loaves and fish. Could he have just as easily upgraded the bread to a better type of bread? Some croissants, maybe? Of course he could have. The question becomes, why didn't he? Maybe it was because sometimes we have to be content with a basic meal, not necessarily a great meal. Part of the toughness of life lately has been readjusting to a basic meal. I had gotten so use to having a meat, three vegetables, rolls, and a dessert that I forgot it doesn't take all of that to meet my need for food.

The people, after they had eaten their fill, got in their minds to take Jesus "by force to make him King" (John 6:15). They were so enamored with what Jesus had done that they wanted him to be their king. He proved he could provide for their needs. They, like us, craved that kind of security—a security that can heal us and provide for our needs. Those of us who have been followers of Christ for a while know how much comfort our hearts take in knowing that Jesus is very concerned with our well-being. He knows the needs in our individual lives, and he has the power to provide them. Many of us could share story after story of how Jesus has provided for us, like these men and women who ate their fill. For some of them, that might have been the first time they had ever literally eaten all they wanted to have.

Jesus perceived that they wanted to make him king by force, so he withdrew to the mountain by himself. Since he went to the mountain alone, we can safely assume, based on other occasions, that he prayed. As he prayed, he would have known as he walked back down that mountain, the tide was about to turn and people would walk away. I pray as his eyes look down on us that we are people who stay with him, learn truths and let them transform us, and go on to live life in the name of Jesus.

The crowd followed Jesus over to Capernaum, and Jesus quickly pointed out to them that they were following him simply because of how they had eaten their fill of the loaves, not because they recognized the signs pointing them to the realization that he was the Christ. They were thrilled to find someone who met their physical needs. This remained their focus. Instead of recognizing and embracing the fullness of the Provider they were stuck concentrating on the provision.

I can see some of that kind of attitude in my own life. As I walk around the garden, my focus has been on my need for some type of security that doesn't change. Maybe my new, desperate search for security is because, for most of my life, some things, like jobs, gas, health insurance, and groceries, have been fairly stable. I didn't recognize how much they were the undergirding of my faith. As the world has shifted, I can see how—like the crowd that followed Jesus that day—much of my devotion to following Jesus has had to do with how much I was able to eat my fill. I, like the Galileans, recognized life's bounties as coming from him, but I still came to him many a morning with a list of needs—actually a list of "needs" that may very well be wants. I'm trying to trade the barley bread Jesus supplies me with for something richer, day after day. Now life is teaching me how blessed I was when I didn't quite recognize it as a blessing. Today I find I'm asking myself, will I be content to have my needs met, or **must** I have my wants also?

Jesus very clearly said to them, "Do not labor for the food that perishes, but for the food that endures to eternal life, which the Son of Man will give you" (John 6:27). These are pretty convicting words when you consider the labor the crowd had just engaged in was following Jesus! How much of my laboring has been for food that perishes? How about you? Can you see how some of your laboring has been for the food that will perish?

The crowd immediately said back to him, "What must we do, to be doing the works of God?" (6:28). Jesus's answer was that they must simply "believe in him whom he [God] has sent" (6:29). Believing in Jesus is the work that will never perish.

Every single time we put our faith in Jesus and believe he is exactly who he said he is, that work will endure forever. In the context of what the Galileans were experiencing, can you sense their struggle?

They had walked a good distance to find Jesus that day. They would have talked about how wonderful it was that Jesus had taken the bread and fish and fed them all! *What a great guy! He is worthy of having us follow him to the ends of the earth.* They did all that just to be told, "You are only seeking me because I fed your belly, not because you really get what I am about."

Jesus went back and forth with them a bit because they started comparing Jesus to Moses and how their forefathers ate manna in the wilderness.

Jesus finally looked at them and states the very first I am statement:

> I am the bread of life; whoever comes to me shall not hunger, and whoever believes in me shall never thirst. But I said to you that you have seen me and yet do not believe. All that the Father gives me will come to me, and whoever comes to me I will never cast out. For I have come down from heaven, not to do my own will but the will of him who sent me. And this is the will of him who sent me, that I should lose nothing of all that he has given me, but raise it up on the last day. For this is the will of my Father, that everyone who looks on the Son and believes in him should have eternal life, and I will raise him up on the last day (John 6:35-40).

The Galileans didn't like it when Jesus told them this. As we read this passage, we may struggle to understand why they were so put out. But what Jesus was saying to them and us is we have to look at him as "the bread of life." The bread (manna) they were trying to compare Jesus to was given to God's people when Moses led them out of Egypt and into the wilderness. If that manna had not fallen, the Israelites would have starved to death. When Jesus took the bread and fish and allowed the people to eat their fill, they saw a chance to have their immediate, physical needs met. Jesus was saying, however, "Forget that earthly bread; I'm all you need." We have said it, heard it, and been taught it, but believing he is all you need is entirely different when you sit down to pay the bills and there isn't enough money, no matter how hard you try.

Jesus was showing the Galileans that they needed to have a long-range viewpoint of life when our human nature is to have a short-range view. Jesus was declaring he had come from heaven in order to feed them what they (and we) truly needed: eternal life.

The people stood around grumbling because they hoped for a political Messiah to meet their immediate, temporary needs, just as I was hoping for a Savior from my financial worries. I came to Jesus with a very limited focal point: today and my needs today.

As we move through the passage of Scripture in John, we find Jesus was about to do what we call around my house "throwing some gas on the fire," and it was going to explode!

"Truly, truly, I say to you, whoever believes has eternal life. I am the bread of life. Your fathers ate the manna in the wilderness, and they died. This is the bread that comes down from heaven, so that one may eat of it and not die. I am the living bread that came down from heaven. If anyone eats of this bread, he will live forever. And the bread that I will give for the life of the world is my flesh." The Jews then disputed among themselves, saying, "How can this man give us his flesh to eat?" So Jesus said to them, "Truly, truly, I say to you, unless you eat the flesh of the Son of Man and drink his blood, you have no life in you. Whoever feeds on my flesh and drinks my blood has eternal life, and I will raise him up on the last day. For my flesh is true food, and my blood is true drink. Whoever feeds on my flesh and drinks my blood abides in me, and I in him. As the living Father sent me, and I live because of the Father, so whoever feeds on me, he also will live because of me. This is the bread that came down from heaven, not like the bread the fathers ate and died. Whoever feeds on this bread will live forever" (John 6:47-58).

On this side of the cross, we can clearly see how Jesus was referring to His crucifixion, but there is more meaning to this passage than simply referring to the cross. We can see two things Jesus said would happen to one who "feeds on his flesh." The first one is one most of us have easily grasped—our belief that Jesus is the Son of God who paid the price for our sins and is now seated at the right hand of God. This belief gives us eternal life. It is the bread we have consumed. We understand that only through Jesus will we see God. It's a onetime decision; we decide to surrender our lives to Jesus, making him Lord of our lives.

The second one was revealed when Jesus said, "Whoever feeds on my flesh and drinks my blood abides in me, and I in him" (John 6:56) This belief implies not only a onetime decision but also a decision that abides and even grows as we consume more of the bread of life—Jesus—throughout our lives.

The crowd labored by following Jesus to where he was, but Jesus told them not to seek him just for earthly things but to focus on the eternal, imperishable work of God, to believe in Jesus. As he stood there declaring he was the bread they would have to consume in order to have eternal life and eating his flesh would enable him to live in them and they in him, the people had to be shaking their heads. They had just walked a good distance because they believed Jesus could meet their needs, and then he flipped and said, "Forget about your needs. All you really need is me because I can give you eternal life."

They would have been shaking their heads, thinking, *Okay, I believe in you. Now can you feed me?* Maybe some of our spiritual hunger is because we have gotten so good at doing certain things, thinking if we do them we will have our bellies fed. The crowd followed Jesus the best way they knew how, and they were told their focus was wrong. We have a million religious activities we engage in that we hope will cause Jesus to feed us, when in reality he would say the same thing to us. "You are seeking me, not because you saw signs but because you ate your fill of the loaves" (John 6:26). These are hard words. Why are *you* seeking Jesus today?

As I have gone back in my mind to the list of prayers I present to Jesus on an almost daily basis, overwhelmingly the prayers are for earthly, daily needs. Very few that I can think of have this bigger picture in mind of believing in Jesus as the bread of life. All I need is Jesus.

When I woke up this morning, just like most mornings, I tried to pray before I ever got out of bed. It was nothing fancy, just an acknowledgment of Jesus, with a quick prayer for the things I know I need. This morning as I woke up trying to put into practice what I have been learning, I was reminded of the Lord's Prayer:

> Our Father in heaven, hallowed be your name. Your kingdom come, your will be done, on earth as it is in heaven. Give us this day our daily bread, and forgive us our debts, as we also have forgiven our debtors. And lead us not into temptation, but deliver us from evil (Matthew 6:9-13).

When Jesus was teaching us how to pray, he directed the primary focus be on the kingdom of God. What is the primary focus of God in our day and age? One of God's primary concerns is people who don't know him—people who, if we don't get active in telling them about God's plan of redemption and all he wants for their lives, will face eternity separated from him. Another thing we know God is concerned with is transforming those of us who are his to look more and more like him. As I rolled those words around in my mind, I was thinking, *How does that change my prayer life? How do I begin to focus on the kingdom and not just my list of needs?* How do you think changing focus will impact your prayers?

One thing I immediately thought of was the people in my life who don't know Jesus. Are they at the top of my prayer list? When I pray for my girls, am I more concerned with what I see of their lives with my eyes or what Jesus is refining in the hidden places of their souls? My daughter, Meghan is going off to college in a very short time. As I have been praying for her, I have lifted up every conceivable thing I can imagine she might need, but one thing I can see I have neglected to do is ask God to give me a sense of his plans for her so I can have a part in praying that plan into being.

As we go back to the crowd of people who were listening to Jesus, his words would have been even harder for the crowd to hear because they didn't have a picture of the cross in mind. They would have had to process whether Jesus was actually talking about truly eating his flesh. Thankfully, on this side of the cross, we don't have to wonder about that!

Not only did the crowd discuss what Jesus said, but his disciples and other followers also had to ponder these difficult sayings. We don't know the exact number of people who followed Jesus regularly, but we know that at one time Jesus sent seventy-two out before him (Luke 10:1). As the Galileans grumbled, Jesus looked at them and asked them, "Do you take offense at this?" (John 6:61). It is off-putting, when you are following Jesus, for him to say, "Better check your motives. Are you here for your own needs or because you believe I am all you need?" There is a huge difference in coming to God to have your needs met and in coming to him because he is all you need, and I am just beginning to come face-to-face with this reality. What is the difference to you?

Jesus went on to say, "It is the Spirit who gives life; the flesh is no help at all. The words that I have spoken to you are spirit and life" (John 6:63). Somehow, as we begin to really take into our mindsets that Jesus is the bread of life, we will find more life. We will have a constant awareness that we must be diligent to make sure we are following Jesus for eternal reasons and not simply to meet our earthly needs.

Jesus is concerned with our daily needs so we will be free to focus all our attention on him, not simply be consumed with our daily needs. When Jesus declared he was the bread of life, many disciples and others in the crowds no longer walked with him. In my own life, sometimes the temptation is to lose faith when my life is not going like I want it to and I'm not having *my needs* met. At those times, I often begin to pull back from Jesus. That's what some of the followers of Jesus did at this point in Jesus's ministry.

Jesus looked at those who knew him best and asked, "Do you want to go away as well?" (John 6:67) It's telling that no one jumped up and said, "No, we want to stay with you!" Peter said, "Lord, to whom shall we go? You have the words of eternal life, and we have believed and have come to know, that you are the Holy One of God" (John 6:68-69).

More than likely you're like me and that's your response to life. You may not be overly happy about it, but you know there isn't anywhere else to go. Jesus is our salvation, and we have believed it. Even if we struggle to realize Jesus is all we need, we are going to keep at it. As we walk through life and struggle with our perceived needs, we have to remember that Jesus *is* concerned with our needs, and if he isn't meeting them, maybe it's so our eyes become fixed on the food (needs) that endures to eternal life. In our quest to understand the phrase "in the name of Jesus," how does Jesus's being the bread of life influence you?

One of the most common ways we use the phrase "in the name of Jesus" is in prayer. Learning to see Jesus as the bread of life inspires a renewed sense of eternal needs, not simply temporal needs. As I glance back at my prayer journal, I realize that I have prayed many prayers asking Jesus to fill my belly while having very little focus on the eternal. I know because Jesus fed the crowd, he is also concerned with my physical needs. He wants me, however, to put my labor into things that have eternal significance. I think I have been doing it the opposite way; I have had much more concern with today's needs and have left the eternal to him. It is becoming clearer that I need to have an eternal perspective on a daily basis. How about you?

Questions to think about:

Go back and review your list. Is there anything you would remove? Is there anything you would add?

Think about a time when you were hopelessly desperate. What did you do at the time to resolve the situation? Would you do anything differently today?

When you consider your personal standard of living, how would you answer the following question: How much is enough?

Status Quo Challenge: *What are you going to do differently this week?*

Briefly describe what keeps you up at night.
What are your fears?

CHAPTER 2

I Am the Light of the World

As I sat once again on my back porch, the sunlight made its daily march across the yard this morning, finally landing on the garden. Thankfully, the garden is no longer being plagued by animals; they must have hated the smelly spray as much as I did. As the light hit the plants, I was struck with how many benefits light brings into our lives.

This spring, our power went out several times and stayed off longer than we liked! When we light a candle, it always amazes me how bright the light is when surrounded by darkness. When you think of light, illumination is likely one of the first things to run through your mind. Maybe you think of how light brings heat. I didn't know until I did a little research that light from the sun is a natural antiseptic. Several articles mentioned how light kills germs. While we all know that light makes you feel better all around, I didn't realize it was actually killing germs too. The benefits of light are very evident among the plants in my garden. By chance, do you remember the first thing God spoke into being? He said, "Let there be light" and there was light (Genesis 1:3).

The book of John opens up with an introduction that tells us several truths about Jesus and the light. Realizing that God made light first made me smile as I read the beginning of the book of John. As you read the passage below, take note what you see about life, light, and the Word.

In the beginning was the Word, and the Word was with God, and the Word was God. He was in the beginning with God. All things were made through him, and without him was not anything made that was made. In him was life, and the life was the light of men. The light shines in the darkness, and the darkness has not overcome it. There was a man sent from God, whose name was John. He came as a witness, to bear witness about the light, that all might believe through him. He was not the light, but came to bear witness about the light. The true light, which enlightens everyone, was coming into the world. He was in the world, and the world was made through him, yet the world did not know him. He came to his own, and his own people did not receive him. But to all who did receive him, who believed in his name, he gave the right to become children of God, who were born, not of blood nor of the will of the flesh nor of the will of man, but of God. And the Word became flesh and dwelt among us, and we have seen his glory, glory as of the only Son from the Father, full of grace and truth (John 1:1-14).

Don't let the first "I am" statement slip out of your mind. Jesus stated, "I am the bread of life" (John 6:35). Each I am statement will peel back a layer uncovering our understanding of Jesus, so that by the end of this book, we will have a clearer understanding of the identity of Jesus. When Jesus said, "I am the bread of life" (John 6:35), we made the connection that he is all we need. As we come to him as our inexhaustible source of life, our focus has to be on who he is, not just what he can do.

As the disciples continued following Jesus, the very next I am statement Jesus made was unique in several ways. He said, "I am the light of the world." Light goes all the way back to Genesis, the beginning. When the children of Israel were led out of slavery, it was with light (Exodus 13:21-22). A verse bringing strength to saints through the ages is: "The LORD is my light and my salvation; whom shall I fear?" (Psalm 27:1). The Old Testament became "a lamp to my feet and a light to my path" (Psalm 119:105). Can you see the connection between life, light, and the Word?

These three—life, light, and the Word—are all wrapped up in the flesh of Jesus. In the passage we are about to look at, John 8:12-20, many scholars[2] believe Jesus spoke these words in the Court of Women in the Temple. The Jewish people would have been celebrating the passing of the long, hot summer days, just as we do, when fall starts to arrive. They held a series of festivals, and one had to do with light. This ceremony involved four large stands each holding four golden bowls being placed in the Court of Women. These sixteen golden bowls (which were reached by ladders) were filled with oil and used the worn undergarments of the priest for wicks. When they were lit at night, all of Jerusalem was illuminated. Can you imagine the light shining from Jerusalem's limestone walls? How far away do you suppose those lights could be seen?

As Jesus stood teaching beneath the sixteen bowls of oil, He declared: "I am the light of the world. Whoever follows me will not walk in darkness, but will have the light of life" (John 8:12). I can only imagine how often the people of Jerusalem walked in darkness because they didn't have modern lights. A torch or a candle, while very helpful, doesn't really put off enough light to give you a sense of brightness. Most of us have a touch of fear in the darkness. Some of us have known how darkness seems to bring out the worst of our human nature—our fears, our evil desires, and even the pain of the past. They all seem to come to life in the darkness. As Jesus stood there surrounded by all that light, imagine how the hearts of the people must have craved that kind of security in their lives. Light always brings security where darkness brought fear, and Jesus stated, "I am the light—as bright as you can imagine—of the whole world!"

Of course, the Pharisees had something to say back to him: "You are bearing witness about yourself; your testimony is not true" (John 8:13). Some of us may be able to recognize that we have a tendency to have just a small amount of Pharisee in ourselves. As I have been wrestling with the truth that Jesus is the bread of life and all I need, it's hard not to look at my Bible and say, *Seriously, You're all I need? How is that going to work on a day-to-day basis?* But when I come back at Jesus, I'm acting just like the Pharisees did. They went back and forth with him, wanting him to somehow prove that he was who he said he was: the light of the world, a light that brings healing warmth to our cold hearts, light that brings direction and security.

As I pondered, I realized that I had to make a choice. Did I believe or not that Jesus is exactly that? Did I stand with the Pharisees or with those who believed him? I can't lose sight of the fact that the Pharisees were religious; they just didn't know Jesus. They knew the Old Testament. They memorized it and dedicated their lives to it; they just couldn't believe that the Messiah acted like Jesus did. They clung to the Old Testament, a book of rules, instead of clinging to the one to whom the book pointed: Jesus.

As Jesus stated that he was the light of the world, many believed in him (John 8:30). Jesus didn't really go into a lot of detail about what his being the light of the world meant, possibly because those who were following him had heard him teach on light earlier. When Jesus shared he was the light of the world, he had already told them that they, the disciples, and us as believers are the light of the world. This is the only I am statement that crosses over to us, those who believe. Every other time Jesus says "I am . . ." it is singular to him. Since we share it with him, it must be pretty significant, right?

As we think about what the disciples would have already known about Jesus, I think we will see why he chose to reveal the I am characteristics about himself in the order he did. In Matthew 4:23-25, note all the different ways Jesus interacted with people.

And he went throughout all Galilee, teaching in their synagogues and proclaiming the gospel of the kingdom and healing every disease and every affliction among the people. So his fame spread throughout all Syria, and they brought him all the sick, those afflicted with various diseases and pains, those oppressed by demons, epileptics, and paralytics, and he healed them. And great crowds followed him from Galilee and the Decapolis, and from Jerusalem and Judea, and from beyond the Jordan (Matthew 4:23-25).

A great crowd began to follow Jesus. Since we know this is before the people started turning away from him, what might have been some of the reasons they were following him?

The people were seeing real, live miracles. People they could reach out and touch had been healed of sicknesses, all kinds of diseases, and problems—all healed by Jesus. Do you think the disciples were excited to be a part of something so exciting and visible?

I do. I can't imagine what kind of excited state I would be in if I had been one of the ones following Jesus. The very next thing Jesus did was to go up on the mountain (Matthew 5:1). The disciples come to him, and Jesus began to teach them. Part of what Jesus told them was that they were the light of the world too. Because the Holy Spirit would reside in them and resides in us, we are invited to participate in all that light does. All the benefits of light flow out of our lives when we are walking in the belief that Jesus is exactly who he said he is.

The hardest part for me as I sit watching the light play across the garden is found in Matthew 5:16, "In the same way, let your light shine before others, so that they may see your good works and give glory to your Father who is in heaven." My human nature tries hard to put my faith in Jesus into a religious box. I find myself in situations where I prefer to just follow my religious practices and not engage humanity at large. I don't mind engaging with people like me—people who like to study the Bible, go to church, and help good people. But as my eyes wander back up to Matthew 4:23-25, I see Jesus in the synagogues but also standing smack in the middle of people we might be tempted to stay away from: sick people with all kinds of diseases and pains, people oppressed by demons and every kind of disease and affliction. Jesus walked among not only the people who were religious but also among the general population who were desperate enough to know they needed help.

Our church runs a food pantry where people can come and get groceries. Access to this food is not based on anything but showing up and asking for help. In my mind, it's the closest I can come to the picture of the crowds that followed Jesus. On any given week, about three hundred families come through the doors of our food pantry. There are all different kinds of people. Some are just people like me who need some help. Others have some kind of sickness that not only is causing them physical pain but is wreaking havoc with their finances as well. People who smile and say thank you. People we are happy that we could help. Then there are the people who come who are hard to serve with a smile. They talk rough, maybe even use ugly words. Some are very picky about what we are giving them; some try to take advantage. But the people who work at the food pantry try hard to serve everyone the same way we see Jesus reaching out to the crowd: with great compassion, love, and grace.

Our family sponsors a young man named Onesmus in Uganda, through Compassion International[3]. We have been sponsoring him for the last several years. He happens to share my birthday. One of the very first things I ever wrote to him was about the sun. We both see the same sun every day, and most days, when we walk outside, we can actually feel the sunlight on our arms and face. I wanted him to know that when he walked outside all the way in Uganda and felt that sun, that I felt the same sun rays and would be thinking about him every single time. Many times when that sunlight hits my skin, I smile and pray for a young man I hope knows that Jesus cares, and that I do too—a young man I may never actually see until we are in heaven but one I pray is feeling the light in me all the way around the world.

Jesus, as the light of the world, invites us to be the light in the very houses we live in, the streets we drive on, and the communities we shop in. Basically, everywhere our feet walk is an opportunity for the light in us to spill out and be felt by someone.

This spring, our country had many devastating tornadoes. My little corner of earth was no exception. We had an opportunity to really let our light shine! In the verses Jesus spoke, notice the word "good."

> You are the light of the world. A city set on a hill cannot be hidden. Nor do people light a lamp and put it under a basket, but on a stand, and it gives light to all in the house. In the same way, let your light shine before others, so that they may see your good works and give glory to your Father who is in heaven (Matthew 5:14-16).

In the passage above, the word *good* is *kalos* (Greek). The early church was marked by this *kalos!* A word that means goodness in action During the aftermath of the tornadoes, my church had the opportunity to start to build relationships because of *kalos* (good works).

As our church group helped those whose lives had been impacted by the tornadoes, I stood in the back of a pickup truck, reached down into a trash can (new) filled with ice and water donated by someone, and handed a refreshing drink of water to another volunteer, who passed it to someone in need of that cold drink. Meghan, Katie, and Lauren, my daughters were serving right there beside me, one of my favorite memories. Chad was wielding a chainsaw with many of the men from not only our church, but the community also.

As we handed out the water, the person who received itr didn't care about what I believe, necessarily. He smiled because of our *kalos* (goodness in action). Time after time, those we were helping asked where we were from. "NorthPointe Church," we would say. Some teared up and said, "I won't ever be able to repay you." Those of us on the NorthPointe Church team knew repayment would never be needed. We were simply getting an opportunity to live what we been given by Christ: grace, unmerited favor.

We got the opportunity to let our light shine, and as we handed out water, cut trees, fed people, and hugged them, they saw Jesus in action, and our hearts reaped a harvest.

One other thing about *kalos* is how it is used in 1 Peter 2:12: "Keep your conduct among the Gentiles honorable, so that when they speak against you as evildoers, they may see your good deeds and glorify God on the day of visitation."

The church has been spoken against for being intolerant, hypocritical, self-righteous, and more. (Sounds like the Pharisees, doesn't it?) NorthPointe Church's good deeds during the tornadoes' aftermath may have possibly caused people who normally have zero use for God or Christians to glorify God or maybe even rethink what they know of Christians. Perhaps they have a new sense of a God who is calling out to them.

As Jesus stood in the Court of the Women, his light had been spilling out all over people—flat-out goodness that was seen and felt by an unbelieving world. I wonder if I could heal people, if would I be tempted to only heal those I felt deserved healing. I bet I would. If I'm truthful, I'm tempted now just to help those with whom I am comfortable. That's not being the light of the world; that's being a Pharisee.

Georgia is so hot now that I have moved from sitting in the garden to sitting on a swing under the deck that looks toward the garden. It's one of those places where I feel at rest. I have that type of personality that doesn't relax easily. The swing normally does it, though. As I sit processing through Jesus being the bread of life and the light of the world, one thing struck a chord in my heart—an uncomfortable chord. It's not about me. It's all about Jesus and others. As tough as the last couple of years have been, it's easy to fall into a cycle of focusing on ourselves and our own household. I have a picture in my mind of light spilling out of me onto others and in turn somehow that same light washing over me too—light that brings healing, warmth, visibility, and security.

An invitation has been extended by Jesus. Actually, it's more of a command. You are the light of the world. Are we willing to be faithful to being that light?

My poor prayer journal is undergoing a transformation, slowly but surely. As I have been trying to have more of an eternal perspective, God has revealed that the very next thing to focus on is helping people. I know from my own life that when people reach out to you, that contact can have eternal ramifications. As a very young twenty-year-old, I was pregnant and almost married. My life had spiraled into one many would have been tempted to shy away from, but one of my mom's friends reached out in kindness to me. She simply brought me baked goodies. She came around every so often as my pregnancy progressed. I got married, and a few short months later, I held a baby girl in my arms. At that exact moment, I wanted her life to turn out differently than mine. I wanted her to be able to close her eyes at night and not have tears fall. In the months that followed the birth of my baby girl, my mom's friend continued to be nice. Really, that about sums up what she did. She was nice to a young woman who didn't have anything to give back to her. Because of her and my mom, I ended up going to church. I heard about Jesus, who loved me and would make me a brand-new creation. Jesus changed my life, but her kindness was the light that he used.

People all around us are desperate for hope. We have it. All we have to do is share it! Are you willing? Am I willing?

Knowledge that doesn't cause change in us is useless. After examining what Jesus was saying about us being the light of the world, my heart was pierced. I could see how much of what I have done turned into mainly being for people who are like me, not reaching out to the general world. We are a whole bunch of lights standing around wondering, "Where is the darkness?" As I stepped out of my comfort zone and asked God how I could be more of a light and reach out to people, God reminded me very gently of when I first started writing and why I first put a pen to paper. In the small church I was attending, they also had a food ministry, but one that took meals into people's homes. Some of the people also brought immediate joy to our hearts when we served them. There were others we served because Jesus would. But every week we gave them a tract. Now, depending on your background you may not be familiar with a tract, but basically, it's a small rectangular publication a little larger than a business card, and it seeks to witness to people about Jesus. There's nothing wrong with them, but we seemed to have bought the biggest box of tracts available, which we handed out every week, and it drove me crazy! I couldn't stand the thought of someone getting the tract, reading it, accepting Jesus, and then only getting the same information week after week after week.

I went to our pastor to ask if I could write a letter about his sermon every week. He gave his blessing! I proceeded to write a letter that was one long paragraph and gave no thought to grammar, punctuation, or ease of reading. After a couple of weeks, a lady came to me and asked if she could help me put it in a more readable format. We worked together for a couple of years doing them. Basically, they turned into short devotionals written for the people I saw each week who were in crisis on some level and may not have had much experience with Jesus or the church. My heart was pierced when I remembered how much more concerned I was during that time with the general population compared to now. I spend a lot of my time and effort, hopefully encouraging the body of Christ but not really reaching out to the world. Jesus did both! I find myself investing in the "safer" place, but the darkness is where the light is needed most.

It's time for a change! As of today, our food pantry will now have a letter written for those who patronize it. I pray those who pick them up know Jesus cares for them and that we, the church, do also. What about you? As you have read the first two chapters, have you made any changes? Or maybe your heart is feeling stirred to make some changes and you are looking wide eyed around for Jesus to show exactly what he would have you do. I would love to hear your stories too. My contact information is in the back of the book if you are willing to share them.

The Seven I Am Statements so far . . .

- I am the bread of life—a focus on eternal needs versus temporal needs.
- I am the light of the world—a commitment to others still in darkness versus ourselves.

Questions to think about:

Thinking about your fears, how would the Light ease them?

Is there anything you are clinging onto that is preventing you from seeing the Light?

Is there anything that is blocking your Light from being seen by others?

Status Quo Challenge: How can you get out of your comfort zone this week?

We all have confidants or people that we trust.
Whose voices do you listen to and why?

I Am the Good Shepherd

J esus's "I am" statements are starting to change. The first two were delivered in a very public setting. Every person who was close enough to hear was invited to listen and respond. The first two I am statements dealt very specifically with having our hearts right, first and foremost, and having hearts that are squarely focused on Christ. We need to have hearts that look at the world and not only desire to shine a light in the darkness but actually do so. Scholars estimate that around three months passed between when Jesus said, "I am the light of the world" when he declared, "I am the door of the sheep . . . I am the good shepherd" (John 10:7, 11).

When Jesus revealed this aspect of who he is, it was his last public discourse. How does knowing Jesus revealed these four aspects in public impact their meaning? One impact is to clearly show us what the Christian faith is designed to look like from Christ's perspective. The first two are focused on what Christ desires from us: hearts that realize he is everything and that have awareness of others who are still in darkness, knowing we are called to bring light to their lives. These next two will focus on what Christ does for us and his heart toward us.

Most of us living in the United States have a hard time imagining much to do with shepherds. When I began this book, most of what I knew was from pictures I saw in children's books of men in long robes walking through a meadow with a walking stick; a very solitary existence. When I did a little digging into shepherding[5] in Jesus's day, I found out several things I didn't know. First, shepherds would have been out in the desert, a very hostile environment, and food and water would have been scarce. Sheep were normally kept away from populated areas because of their need to graze and their smell, so in addition to being in an environment where the basic necessities were in short supply, shepherds would have also been out where wild animals roam. In the evening, the shepherd would lead the sheep to the sheep pen. Typically it would have been a rough stone or mud-brick structure that was only partially roofed, if covered at all. The walls would have been around waist high and covered with thorny underbrush, or sometimes it was simply a cave in the hills. It was where the shepherd took the sheep to keep them safe—a place of refuge during the darkness of night, which was the most dangerous part of the day.

The shepherd, after getting the sheep into the pen, would become the door or the gate. Most times the shepherd simply lay down in the doorway so nothing could get in or past him. Because of the environment, it wasn't unusual for several shepherds to share one pen. A shepherd would stand at the doorway and inspect each sheep as it walked through. He would look to make sure the sheep had no injuries from being in the hostile environment. He would have noticed any scrapes, thorns, or broken bones because of his close inspection. He would offer the sheep a drink of water. A shepherd also talked to his sheep and normally played some music from his instrument, like a flute. He would develop his own melody. He played often enough for the sheep that they identified the melody with care and companionship. Because of his care and their repeated exposure to his voice and the melodies, the sheep would follow him anywhere.

Each morning when the shepherds would leave the pen, each shepherd would play his own personal tune, and his sheep would follow him out into the desert. They knew his voice so well that they could distinguish it from the voices any other shepherds who might have been sharing the same sheep pen. The sheep trusted their shepherd. They knew he would lead them as safely as he could, and if they were somehow injured, they knew he would tend to their wounds with the utmost care.

Our own hostile environment we have to venture out into on a daily basis resembles the desert. I listened to the news this morning, and several of the stories just made me shake my head in sadness, with a tinge of fear, especially as I thought of my three daughters who are making their way in the world. We may not fear literal wild animals on a daily basis, but we would be wise to acknowledge that we are surrounded by a world that has people who are cruel and heartless. We live in an environment where two of the most basic necessities are in short supply: being loved and feeling secure. As you read John 10:1-10, notice what else we need to be aware of.

"Truly, truly, I say to you, he who does not enter the sheepfold by the door but climbs in by another way, that man is a thief and a robber. But he who enters by the door is the shepherd of the sheep. To him the gatekeeper opens. The sheep hear his voice, and he calls his own sheep by name and leads them out. When he has brought out all his own, he goes before them, and the sheep follow him, for they know his voice. A stranger they will not follow, but they will flee from him, for they do not know the voice of strangers." This figure of speech Jesus used with them, but they did not understand what he was saying to them. So Jesus again said to them, "Truly, truly, I say to you, I am the door of the sheep. All who came before me are thieves and robbers, but the sheep did not listen to them. I am the door. If anyone enters by me, he will be saved and will go in and out and find pasture. The thief comes only to steal and kill and destroy. I came that they may have life and have it abundantly."

A thief and a robber, at a casual glance, may seem to be the same thing—someone who steals. But how they do their crime is very different. A thief deals with subtlety and trickery. I think of people who are pickpockets. They can take your wallet without you even knowing it! Or I think of the people who can spin an elaborate tale and we fall for it. A robber, on the other hand, uses violence and fear to steal from you.

Jesus is telling us people are going to come into our lives and try to convince us to follow them. They may do it very subtly, with words that sound like music to our ears. Others are going to come into our lives with violence and fear and demand we follow them. I'm putting a very real and human face to this, but Jesus reminds us in John 10:10, "The thief comes only to steal and kill and destroy. I came that they may have life and have it abundantly." While it may be a human face we gaze into, we have to remember Satan is the true thief and robber whose desire is nothing more than to destroy us. He'll use whatever means works, whether it is subtle trickery or a full onslaught of terror. However, if we recognize the voice of our shepherd and stay close to him, we will spare ourselves untold pain.

Where I am seeing this play out so vividly in my own life right now is in the lives of my daughters. They go to a public middle school, high school and one is now in college, and like most teens, they are very active on Facebook. Because of their ages—nineteen, fifteen, and thirteen—I have my eyes glued to their status updates and their friends' updates. Like most of us, they have their closest friends, people they know fairly well, and people they barely know as part of their friends' list. Between the three of them and my own friends' list, it's almost like I have my own research group available. They, and even myself at times, are often exposed to status updates that can subtly trick them into following the wrong voice. One I found myself falling for, was when people put a certain T.V. show *is wonderful!* Several times I would believe them, put it on and quickly realize it was garbage. The world is telling us all kinds of garbage and whispers it so sweetly, coaxing us that if only we will do this or that, we will have all our hearts desire. Or the world uses strong-arm tactics, hoping for the same result—that we will follow that voice down a path that leads to destruction. Jesus was giving his listeners, and us, a wake-up call when he declared, "I am the good shepherd." That statement reminds us we have to spend enough time with the shepherd to memorize his voice. If we don't, we will follow any voice.

At night let's remember that as we imagine ourselves walking through the door Jesus is inspecting us for any hurts from the day and is ready to bandage them. He is standing with a drink of refreshing water if we are weary from being out in the hostile environment. He has a kind word on his lips that says, "You are loved and cared for." Of course, by implication that would mean when our eyes open, we realize Jesus stands at the door ready to lead us out into the desert.

I have an image in mind of sheep being led out as opposed to cattle being driven. A sheep follows the shepherd; the shepherd knows where the water is, where green grass is growing, and exactly where there is a shade tree to rest under. He also knows where the sheep pen is at night so the sheep will be safe. The sheep follow him willingly. Not so much with a cattle drive. A cattle drive was designed to get the cattle to go from point A to point B, normally to slaughter the cattle. Cowboys rode behind them with a bullwhip to keep them in line. It also took several cowboys to drive the cattle from one place to another. This is a sharp contrast to a sheep.

Jesus goes on to say in addition to being the door, he is also the "good shepherd." Basically, there are two types of shepherds: those who own the sheep and those who are hired to watch them. I think of King David as being a shepherd whose family owned the sheep. A couple of years ago, we went from owning a home to renting a home. When we were renting, our attitude was a little different than when we owned the home. The house we were renting was brand new. It was in a subdivision where a builder had several homes he couldn't sell, so he was forced to try to rent them. It was very pretty, and we felt very blessed to be able to rent a new home.

But right after we moved in, we noticed in the living room that one of the walls had a crack in it—the kind of crack that occurs when the house settles a bit. Then a few weeks later, we noticed the front porch steps were cracking. While we looked at the cracks and knew somewhere down the road they might develop into a problem, we didn't actually do anything about it. Our commitment level to the house was low. We knew at some point we would move on to another house. Our plan was to have our own home that we felt responsible for and cared for it because it was "ours." For example, when we bought our house that we live in now, we noticed the gutters on the house needed to be cleaned out. Within days, we were on a ladder cleaning out the gutters. Just yesterday Chad mentioned we were going to have to clean the gutters again.

Both the cracks and the gutters represent the same thing in my mind: an awareness we had of a situation that could turn into a problem. But our response was vastly different. A hired shepherd, like we were as renters, might look at the sheep and notice the problem, but he lacks the commitment of the one who owns the sheep. Another difference is in how you react when trouble comes to your door. In shepherding, sometimes when a wild animal would come, a shepherd would throw it a lamb to run away to either save himself or the rest of the flock. We still hear the saying, "Like a lamb thrown to the wolves." I don't think I have ever thought about who was doing the throwing. Have you? Obviously it couldn't be the other sheep. Only the shepherd had the ability to throw the lamb to a wolf. If you watch the news, you may recall seeing some of the country that has been facing unprecedented floods. Many homeowners stayed to protect their homes to the best of their abilities, but never did I see a renter say he or she was staying. Trust me, when we were renting, if we had been faced with a flood, we would have packed up and left. The commitment difference is huge. Christ, as our shepherd, sees us as his and was willing to lay down his life for us.

As you read the last of what Jesus said, keep in mind this was his last public lesson. See if you can pick up a new theme in his words.

I am the good shepherd. The good shepherd lays down his life for the sheep. He who is a hired hand and not a shepherd, who does not own the sheep, sees the wolf coming and leaves the sheep and flees, and the wolf snatches them and scatters them. He flees because he is a hired hand and cares nothing for the sheep. I am the good shepherd. I know my own and my own know me, just as the Father knows me and I know the Father; and I lay down my life for the sheep. And I have other sheep that are not of this fold. I must bring them also, and they will listen to my voice. So there will be one flock, one shepherd. For this reason the Father loves me, because I lay down my life that I may take it up again. No one takes it from me, but I lay it down of my own accord. I have authority to lay it down, and I have authority to take it up again. This charge I have received from my Father (John 10:11-18).

This is really the first we see of Jesus saying he is planning to bring Gentiles into the sheep pen. One flock, one shepherd. I was telling Katie, my middle daughter, how much better churches do with this concept compared to even fifteen years ago. Most churches have become very interconnected with one another, and rightly so. Jesus is what binds us together, and the other shouldn't be able to divide us.

If we try to pull these four I am statements together as the public expression of Christ, what do they tell us?

- I am the bread of life—a focus on eternal needs verses temporal needs.
- I am the light of the world—a commitment to others still in darkness versus ourselves.
- I am the door of the sheep—Jesus's focus on us and the care he shows us daily.
- I am the good shepherd—Jesus's commitment to us is 100 percent. He will never throw us to the wolves.

I can see how living life "in the name of Jesus" changes me as I have become more aware of how Jesus described himself.

Some of the changes are painful; my heart is drawn daily to focus on temporal needs.

Being willing to take our light out into the darkness is going to bring some insecurity into our hearts and maybe some fear. But just like the sheep, we have to know we are following the shepherd and he is leading us through it. He is not behind us, driving us out into the darkness, but right out there in front of us to guide us and protect us.

As we focus our hearts firmly on Christ and his eternal work, we know his invitation to us to be the light of the world is going to require us to step out of the sheep pen and into a hostile environment. Our environment is going to injure us, either when we drift too far away from our shepherd or when the terrain is so hard that even following Jesus closely will result in a few scratches to our hearts and minds. At the end of the day, we have to follow Jesus back to the sheep pen, where he can anoint our wounds with oil to heal them, where he can give us a drink of water, and where we can lay our heads down, knowing our shepherd guards us. Psalm 23 is a beautiful picture of what we have been discussing.

> The LORD is my shepherd; I shall not want. He makes me lie down in green pastures. He leads me beside still waters. He restores my soul. He leads me in paths of righteousness for his name's sake. Even though I walk through the valley of the shadow of death, I will fear no evil, for you are with me; your rod and your staff, they comfort me. You prepare a table before me in the presence of my enemies; you anoint my head with oil; my cup overflows. Surely goodness and mercy shall follow me all the days of my life, and I shall dwell in the house of the LORD forever (Psalm 23).

When we first started this journey I was worried my garden wouldn't produce enough of a harvest to do anything with. Now I'm thinking, *What am I going to do with all those tomatoes?* On some level I have seen what we are learning playing out in my garden. In my little garden, I'm the shepherd of it; okay, really it would be my husband, Chad, more than me, but just play along. The first thing we had to focus on was the animals eating it. We put a net up, and we sprayed the perimeter with stink. Then as it began to grow, we had to water it, fertilize it, keep the bugs off, and tend to it. But because of our care, we are seeing food that we can pick and eat. We are seeing "fruit" from our work.

Seeing the example from the garden encourages me to realize that just as we walked around that little patch of earth, trying to protect it and give it the things it needs to flourish, Jesus is doing the same thing to my life and yours. If we let him refocus our hearts to more eternal matters and our eyes to the darkness around us, his eyes will be so closely glued to us when we walk through the door of the sheep pen each day that he'll stand ready to soothe any scratches we have sustained. He'll remove any thorns from us before they turn into an infected mess. When we are parched because life in the desert has been tough, he'll offer us a drink of water to refresh our weary hearts. Any enemies that dare to come after us will first meet him. All of this is only possible if we will realize as sheep our responsibility is to learn our shepherd's voice and to follow him where he leads us.

I'm excited we are moving from Jesus's public ministry into a very intimate setting as he reveals more of who he is. I can't wait until we start exploring what our new awareness of who Jesus is will bring to our lives as we start to see the power wrapped up in the name of Jesus. We already know he desires for that power to change our light from a light bulb to floodlight in our very own corners of desert living!

The Seven I Am Statements so far . . .

- I am the bread of life—a focus on eternal needs versus temporal needs.
- I am the light of the world—a commitment to others still in darkness versus ourselves.
- I am the door of the sheep—Jesus's focus on us and the care he shows us daily.
- I am the good shepherd—Jesus's commitment to us is 100 percent. He will never throw us to the wolves.

Questions to think about:

Remembering who you listen to, are they the voice of a shepherd?

Think about a time you followed someone or something that turned out to be a mistake. What was it and why did you follow?

What in your life would you throw to the wolves?

Status Quo Challenge: What will you commit to this week?

Have you ever experienced any
miracles in your life?

I Am the Resurrection
and the Life

Do you remember at the beginning of our journey when I shared that I cried in the garden, overwhelmed by life? I cried alone that day. I'm not a big crier by nature, and if I do cry, most of the time it's when I am alone. That morning when I walked into my house from the garden, my feelings stayed with me—anger, fear, anxiety, loss, and loneliness. My crying did bring me to a place where I started searching God's Word for answers, but the feelings lingered longer than usual.

Recently, I was walking with two friends, Carrie and Laura, pouring out my heart about a situation with one of my daughters. I had gone past the point of telling them what was going on in the situation and moved to how I felt about the situation. When I described how I felt, I had to use a very different set of words and emotions. As long as I focused on what was going on, my emotions stayed in check, but when I opened up about how it was making me feel, those emotions poured out, unchecked and unwelcomed. I cried the ugly cry.

We stopped right in the middle of the trail we were walking in our community park, and Carrie said, "We need to pray." At the same time, my other friend, Laura, was looking around for some place a little more private than the middle of the trail. She saw that after a couple of more steps, we would top the hill, and she knew there was a bench there. She started yelling,

"Bench, bench." The only trouble was, both my friend and I misunderstood her, and we thought she was calling me an ugly name. We both looked at her in shock. I was thinking, *How could she call me that? Is it because of what I'm feeling?*

Poor Laura—as we looked at her like she had two heads, she was thinking, *What is wrong with wanting to get out of the way of everybody else walking and then praying?*

After we realized she was saying bench, between crying and laughing, we were a sight to see! I sat down on the bench, and they prayed for me while I cried. After that, I felt better. The emotions were still there, but they were not raging.

After our walk, I came home and started cleaning the kitchen. As I washed the dishes, I told God I didn't understand why he wasn't fixing this situation. Why? Where was he? Did he not love me as much as I thought he did? I thought I had cried the ugly cry with my friends, but it was nothing compared to the crying going on in my kitchen. At one point I had a big, white plastic bowl in my hands, and I wanted nothing more than to squeeze it hard enough to shatter it in a million pieces.

I poured out the whole gamut of negative emotions there at the sink, bowl in hand—all my frustration, anger, and sadness.

When I finally looked down at the bowl I was squeezing in a death grip, I realized all those feelings were swirling down the drain, and what I was left with was a heart ready to hear from God.

As I walked into my living room to do some research on the next "I am" statement of Jesus, I didn't know he was about to walk right into my situation. You see, that's the beauty of Jesus; nothing draws him to us like a hurting heart poured out before him, ready to hear his voice.

Jesus began to remind me of the setting for our next I am statements, a very private setting with those who loved him. He did not reveal them to the masses of people who claimed to know him but to the ones who stayed even when life was crashing in all around their heads. Maybe you're like me and that's the way your life is going too. I know as we lean in close, our hearts poured out before him, Jesus is going to speak right into our situations.

In John 11, we find Lazarus sick, so his sisters, Martha and Mary, sent word to Jesus to come, saying, "Lord, he whom you love is ill" (v. 3). I have been doing that same thing; have you too? I have been sending word to Jesus that the one he loves is ill for the last year. Martha and Mary expected the same thing we do: for Jesus to respond and come—quickly, I might add.

But Jesus didn't come when they called. He actually stayed where he was for two more days—two long, hard, emotional days where the sisters looked up and didn't see him coming. During those two days, they buried Lazarus, the brother they loved. Jesus, they knew, could have healed their brother without even coming to them. Jesus could have spoken the words, and Lazarus would have been healed. Jesus had done it before (Matthew 8:5-13).

I wonder if, as Martha and Mary sat at Lazarus's bedside, they searched his face, looking for something to happen at the moment Jesus heard of his illness. As they watched him get sicker and sicker, how their minds must have begin to doubt everything they thought they knew about Jesus. I wonder when they began to start to wonder if Jesus didn't really love them, maybe they had just been part of the group. When did they realize no healing was going to take place? As Lazarus died and the tears started to roll, do you think they had the same emotions we do?

You better believe they did! If we looked at other places where Martha and Mary's lives are retold, we would find Martha having no trouble telling Jesus to do something about her lazy (in her eyes) sister! We could also see Mary going into a room of men to hear from the Teacher, even if it made the men uncomfortable and her sister mad (see Luke 10:38-42).

Just like us, I'm sure Martha and Mary started looking for Jesus to do something as soon as he heard their message. Rightly so, we want to be people who believe God answers prayers. The trouble comes when Jesus delays.

When Jesus got close enough to Bethany, Martha ran out to meet him. I love what she says: "Lord, if you had been here, my brother would not have died. But even now I know that whatever you ask from God, God will give you" (John 11:21-22). Martha was clear headed in her approach to Jesus. She knew he could have saved Lazarus, and she even knew Jesus could bring him back even now, even though he was already dead and buried. I wonder if, like us, she had the head knowledge. We know God can do anything and nothing is too hard for him, but we *don't really expect him* to do something miraculous.

Or had she been reminding herself of when Jesus had brought someone back from the dead? Did she think of the daughter of Jairus, who died while Jesus was on the way to her house, only to arise, hungry when Jesus walked in and took her hand? (Mark 5:21-43).

Did Martha remind herself of the young man Jesus raised from the dead when he saw the boy's mother crying? Jesus had compassion on her, reached out, and brought the young man back to life (Luke 7:11-15). Was Martha hoping for a similar response? I don't know what Martha was thinking, but we do know when she met Jesus, she approached him in all of his divinity, all of his power, and all of his glory!

Jesus responded back to her faith by saying, "I am the resurrection and the life. Whoever believes in me, though he die, yet shall he live, and everyone who lives and believes in me shall never die. Do you believe this?"

Martha answered, "Yes, Lord; I believe . . ." (John 11:25-27).

Martha walked back home, knowing that one day she would see her brother again. Sometimes when Jesus comes into our situations, we know, like Martha, he can do a very present-day miracle, but we walk home knowing our miracle of seeing our situation fixed will come later. The divine nature of Jesus and the ways of God don't always make sense to us. We want to receive the miracle in the moment every time we call out. But in reality, sometimes Jesus is going to say, "I will fix it, eventually. Do you trust me?"

Yes, Lord. I believe.

We walk home, often not knowing our eyes are about to see a miracle much sooner than we thought. We just know Jesus says he has it handled.

When Martha walked into the house, she told Mary, "The teacher is calling for you." Mary was up and out the door! People went out to follow her, thinking she was going to weep at the tomb. Martha and Mary said pretty much the exact same words to Jesus: "Lord, if you had been here, my brother would not have died" (v. 32).

Martha went to Jesus in his divinity: "I know that whatever you ask from God, God will give you." Mary, on the other hand, approached Jesus in his humanity. She fell at his feet weeping. When Jesus saw her weeping, he was deeply moved in his spirit and greatly troubled (v. 33). Jesus wept (v. 35). He was fully God and fully human, all at the same time.

As we seek to apply these "I am" statements to our lives, this calamity illustrates Jesus's perfect divine nature and fully human nature that are not in conflict with one another but that give us another wonderful gift. We are invited to approach God's throne, knowing that our Priest, Jesus, is able to sympathize with our weaknesses because he has felt the same emotions.

"Let us then with confidence draw near to the throne of grace, that we may receive mercy and find grace to help in time of need" (Hebrews 4:16).

As I studied this scene of Mary crying while I sat in my living room where I have cried many tears, it connected the dots in my heart to my own ugly cry. When I cry alone, other than the natural release one feels with a good cry, nothing happens. When I cry with others, I not only get the natural release but also the comfort human hands bring. But when I cry with Jesus (notice I said *with* Jesus) and go to him, falling at his feet crying, he is moved with compassion. He loves us. The eternal plan of God and the compassion of our fully human Savior somehow meet when we pour out our hearts.

Life has been hard the last few years, and I have felt this disconnect from what my head knows and what my heart feels. I have been overly focused on the divine nature of Jesus when sometimes what I really need is the human side. I need to know that when I cry, Jesus isn't looking down from a throne high above. He is right there with me, remembering what those emotions feel like to us humans, and his heart is moved.

If you're familiar with the story, you know that Jesus did bring Lazarus back from the dead. Both Martha and Mary saw the miracle they had longed for from the moment they first sent word back to Jesus. In my own life, reading this passage, my heart is greatly encouraged. Even though I haven't seen the miracle yet, I know more clearly than ever how Jesus feels as he looks at my situation. He feels deeply moved, greatly troubled, and ready to call with a loud voice, "Lazarus, come out."

Jesus's public revealing of his names showed us his mission, but the private names show us the heart of Christ:

- I am the Bread of Life shows a focus on eternal needs versus temporal needs.
- I am the Light of the World shows a commitment to others rather than ourselves.
- I am the Door of the sheep shows Jesus's focus on us.
- I am the Good Shepherd shows Jesus's commitment to us.
- I am the Resurrection and the Life shows Jesus's divinity and humanity coming together to give us life both here on earth and in heaven.

Most of the time I'm prone to focus on the miracle of a dead person coming back to life, but sometimes what I need in my life more than anything is to know that even when Jesus delays responding to my first cry, it's not because he doesn't care; it's only because he has a greater miracle planned.

Maybe like me, you've been calling out and watching the horizon for Jesus to show up, but the situation continues to deteriorate. Maybe, like Mary and Martha, you don't understand why _____ has been happening. Pour out your heart to him, tell him you know he can fix the situation, and tell him exactly how you feel. We may not get up knowing exactly what he is going to do, but we will know without a shadow of a doubt that we are cared for deeply.

Two more times Jesus will say, "I am," and two more times our hearts will be enriched with new knowledge and understanding! With that knowledge and understanding, we will turn our eyes to the book of Acts, where people were living a roller coaster existence much like ours. I can't wait to see how they lived this knowledge and understanding out. More importantly, I can't wait to see what it does in our own lives!

The Seven I Am Statements so far . . .

- I am the bread of life—a focus on eternal needs versus temporal needs
- I am the light of the world—a commitment to others still in darkness versus ourselves
- I am the door of the sheep—Jesus's focus on us and the care he shows us daily
- I am the good shepherd—Jesus's commitment to us is 100 percent. He will never throw us to the wolves.
- I am the resurrection and the life—Jesus's divinity and humanity coming together to give us life both here on earth and in heaven.

Questions to think about:

Looking back at the miracles you experienced, were you expecting them to happen? Did you see them for what they were at the time? If not, what prevented you from seeing them?

Are you waiting for a miracle right now? What is it?

Has there ever been a time that your "clear head" got in the way of your faith? What was it?

Status Quo Challenge: What will you share with Jesus this week?

We have all heard bad news at one time or another. Think of a time you received heartbreaking news from someone you cared about. What thoughts immediately went through your head at the time?

CHAPTER 5

I Am the Way, the Truth and the Life

I went down in the basement and I noticed that my jars of squash I had canned during the summer had problems to say the least. They were a beautiful yellow color when I carried them to the basement and now they were brown with fuzzy stuff growing on them. As I walked over to the jars I was wondering what in the world I had done wrong. It didn't take me but a minute to remember after I took the jars out of the canner I had taken the rings off the jars, I was sure the seal would hold. I was also wrong. The jars had let air in and they had each spoiled. I felt betrayed by my squash. All that work, all that effort I had put into them and they still spoiled. Now, in my mind the squash were more responsible for spoiling than my lack of properly following directions. But we'll let that point go, won't we?

Can you even imagine how Jesus must have felt as he sat at the table during the Last Supper looking around and being troubled in his spirit (John 13:21), he knew one seated with him—Judas—was about to betray him. The disciples were sitting around the table trying to keep up with what was going on. Jesus was saying someone would betray him and that very shortly he would also be leaving them. The emotions of the disciples must have been all over the place. Just imagine for a second having Jesus scan the room while saying, "Someone here is going to betray me." I know if I heard him say it, I would be thinking. *Not me. Surely not me. Please not me.* Then a few minutes later Jesus said, "Where I'm going you cannot follow me" (John 13:36).

Peter was quick to say, "Lord, why can I not follow you now? I will lay down my life for you" (v. 37). Jesus basically answered, "No, Peter, actually in addition to being betrayed tonight by Judas, I will have to endure you denying me three times before the night is over" (paraphrase).

By this point, the disciples' whole world revolved around Jesus, and he told them he was leaving and they couldn't go but they were to love one another. Love one another? They had just been arguing about who the greatest was! (See Luke 9:46.) Their heads had to be spinning. They must have been perplexed and maybe even a little fearful. It was in this atmosphere of confusion and fear where Jesus revealed another I am statement.

Personally, my head has some confusion and fear circling around in it also. Even as we have been learning about who Jesus says he is, that knowledge has been causing my head to go round and round in circles, trying to figure out how to apply it to my daily life: Don't be overwhelmingly concerned with temporal needs, Jenny. Remember, I am the Bread of Life (John 6:35). I am the Light of the World. Take my light, Jenny, and get out into the darkness (John 8:12). Trust that as you go out into the darkness, I will lead you. I'm a Good Shepherd. Whatever you need, I will provide. Only learn my voice and follow me (John 10:9-11). I am the Resurrection and the Life. My humanity and divinity make me what your heart yearns for: a perfect Savior who knows how you feel (John 11:25-26).

Jesus is going to speak right into the disciple's hearts with words many of us have quoted: "I am the way, and the truth, and the life. No one comes to the Father except through me" (John 14:6). But for our purposes, we have to go a bit deeper in the passage to really pull the meaning out of this I am statement.

> "If you had known me, you would have known my Father also. From now on you do know him and have seen him." Philip said to him, "Lord, show us the Father, and it is enough for us." Jesus

said to him, "Have I been with you so long, and you still do not know me, Philip? Whoever has seen me has seen the Father. How can you say, 'Show us the Father'? Do you not believe that I am in the Father and the Father is in me? The words that I say to you I do not speak on my own authority, but the Father who dwells in me does his works. Believe me that I am in the Father and the Father is in me, or else believe on account of the works themselves. Truly, truly, I say to you, whoever believes in me will also do the works that I do; and greater works than these will he do, because I am going to the Father. Whatever you ask in my name, this I will do, that the Father may be glorified in the Son. If you ask me anything in my name, I will do it" (John 14:7-14).

It makes my head spin trying to learn what Jesus was saying and how we can apply it. Can you imagine being in the room with him? If you are like me, when you see those last two verses, your entire focus falls there: "Whatever you ask in my name, this I will do . . . if you ask me anything in my name, I will do it." Do you mentally shake your head and wonder what that means? If you're like me, maybe you even wonder why it doesn't work. Those words are hard to swallow. Why did Jesus say we would do even greater works than him and that whatever we asked in his name he'd do, but then we live life without either being our reality?

As I have been living life the last few years, this has become the crux of the matter. Where is the power that I see Jesus promising here? When we turn our eyes to the book of Acts, this was the people of the early church's reality.

As we have gone through six of the "I am" statements, I know one problem I have is a very self-centered belief system. When Jesus looked at the crowd and said they only followed him because he fed their bellies (John 6:26), my heart was broken, because in prayer after prayer, I have sought to have my belly filled. My light prefers to hang out where there are plenty of other lights. Jesus was telling them and us that we would continue his work, and when we had needs in context of doing his work, all we had to do was ask. Do you see the same difference I do? How many times have I prayed only for very short-lived temporal wants versus prayers where the overall goal is to share love in some way? Jesus didn't just do the miracles but also deeds of humility, service, and love.

It's becoming crystal clear that Jesus was promising great power to those who would continue what he started—reaching out to a world with grace and love—not so much power in temporal areas. Once I started understanding the back story of all these statements, then when Jesus says he is the way, the truth, and the life, they started coming together.

Jesus is the only way to the Father, but he is also the truth and the life. Each of them is singular to him. He is the only way to God, but our society struggles with such an exclusive claim. Many view all the religious systems as variations of the same theme. But he said very clearly he is it—the only way. Not only does he teach truth but he also embodies truth. He doesn't represent life; he is the life. This truth can't be compromised because God himself was Christ. Christ wasn't created; he was, he is, and he will be.

> In the beginning was the Word, and the Word was with God, and the Word was God. He was in the beginning with God . . . In him was life and the life was the light of men . . . And the Word became flesh and dwelt among us . . . (John 1:1-2, 4, 14).

As soon as Jesus said, "If you ask me anything in my name, I will do it," he immediately said, "If you love me, you will keep my commandments" (14:15). Before this he stated, "A new commandment I give to you, that you love one another: just as I have loved you . . ." (13:34). He knows our focus is always going to be torn between having a temporal view and an eternal view, so the Father gave us another "Helper, to be with us forever, even the Spirit of truth . . ." (14:16-17).

This is the introduction to the Holy Spirit, the Spirit of truth. The Holy Spirit is the one Jesus said would teach the disciples all things and bring to their remembrance all that Jesus said (14:26). The Spirit went on to empower the early church, so for us this is of huge importance because we are trying to learn to live life like the early believers did. This introduction to the Holy Spirit came in a time when the disciples had to have heads that were spinning!

Jesus was promising them they would understand as the days went on. We as believers under the New Covenant already are benefiting from having the Holy Spirit in us. As we look on these passages, much is clearer to us than it was to them.

If I stopped right now, what I have already learned has vastly changed my head, but my heart is still processing it. The other night I stood before a group of women, and as my mouth opened to pray for them, the words coming out reflected a much more eternal view. I felt more confident in the words because I knew they were based out of an understanding—a new understanding for me—of how much more important the eternal is. At the same time, the situation with my daughter I mentioned in the last chapter weighs heavy on my heart. How do we move from having temporal prayers to prayers that reflect the eternal mission of Jesus's love even in the day-to-day struggles of life?

I started asking myself, "Which portion of this struggle is temporal, and which portion has eternal consequences?" As I have been praying over this situation, one of the temporal sides that has come forward is pride—my pride. I don't want to deal with this situation because of my pride. I would prefer for it to have never happened or for Jesus to make it all better immediately! How do I pray and somehow remove the pride from my heart? I know any prayer rooted in pride isn't going to be one I will see Jesus answering, regardless of whether I pray it in his name or not.

If I'm being honest, I can acknowledge in my situation that my prayers are all tangled up between the eternal and the temporal. I can see the eternal portion, but honestly, the temporal holds me tightly in its grip. I'm praying you are wrestling through these same kinds of thoughts. For me, becoming aware of them has been a huge step. If we are going to have the power to live life in the name of Jesus as the early church did, we have to be willing to change.

The disciples had to confront their feelings and make the choice to believe that Jesus is the way, the truth, and the life. He is a way paved by love, truth expressed through love, and life that demonstrates love even now. The temporal loses when confronted with love and causes the eternal to win. But what a struggle it is.

I can't overlook how significant the Holy Spirit moving from being on someone to being "in" us is in our lives. During Old Testament times the Holy Spirit would come "on" someone, but would leave for different reasons. (1 Samuel 16:14) When Jesus tells the disciples and us, the Holy Spirit would be in us 'forever' can you imagine the security that must have flooded their minds? I wonder if, as the disciples stood there taking in all these words, if they were struck with how different what their thoughts had been and what Jesus was saying here. The Holy Spirit dwelling within believers gives us access to power that no one had ever experienced before. A power, where fear of disappointing God would cause the Spirit to leave has been removed as a possibility. The Spirit also brings clarity as we study the Bible and supplies the power to live it out. What a difference the Holy Spirit makes to our lives as we begin to depend on him more and more.

The Seven I Am Statements

- I am the bread of life—a focus on eternal needs versus temporal needs.

- I am the light of the world—a commitment to others still in darkness versus ourselves.

- I am the door of the sheep—Jesus's focus on us and the care he shows us daily.

- I am the good shepherd—Jesus's commitment to us is 100 percent. He will never throw us to the wolves.

- I am the resurrection and the life—Jesus's divinity and humanity coming together to give us life both here on earth and in heaven.

- I am the way, the truth, and the life—Jesus is the only way, the only truth, and the only life worth living.

Questions to think about:

Going back to the bad news you received. Were your prayers answered? What happened?

How would we know if our belief system was self-centered or not? Are there any indicators that we could identify?

Describe a time when the Spirit was **in** you.

Status Quo Challenge: How will my prayers change this week?

What does the word obedience mean to you?

I Am the True Vine

I sat in a restaurant today and talked with a friend about the power of the Holy Spirit in our lives. We talked about what made some people *seem* like they are super-Christians while we aren't. We talked through all kinds of reasons, and we finally boiled it down to one thing: obedience. The one thing that is the hardest for this heart of mine to do—simply obeying—is what has the power to transform my life. It will be a transformation from sitting in a garden, crying and feeling overwhelmed, to a life where even as the world rapidly shifts, my eyes will stay focused on the unchanging truth of the Word of God. As we begin looking at the last I am statement Jesus made, we be called to obedience. The funny thing is, we get to make the choice to what degree. Will we become people who act on what they know or not?

Jesus said, "If you ask me anything in my name, I will do it" (John 14:14) after he said he is the way, the truth, and the life. Then he immediately starts talking about the Holy Spirit. The Holy Spirit is our helper in life—the one who will teach us and bring to our remembrance all that Jesus has said (John 14:26). I pulled out the best part of this section, the part most of us are comfortable with. But intermingled with these verses are words like "If you love me, you will keep my commandments" (John 14:15) and "Whoever has my commandments and keeps them, he it is who loves me" (John 14:21). Two more times in this same passage Jesus says love means we will keep his commandments.

I wonder how many times the Holy Spirit has brought to my remembrance what Jesus says about something and I chose to do it my own way. If you could get in my face in those moments and ask me, "Jenny, do you love Jesus?" what would I answer? What would you answer?

The last two I am statements are revealed in the same time period, right before the arrest of Jesus. Really it's only hours away. As Jesus looked at his disciples' faces, he was sharing the most intimate moment with them, and us, that I can imagine. He knew very soon their worlds would be turned upside down, tears would flow, and they would feel so lost. Imagine what you would say to your friends and your family if you knew it would be the last conversation you would have with them before you were crucified—not just killed but publically crucified. All the fluff would disappear, and all that your heart would want to convey to them is the absolute truth you wanted them to wake thinking about. I picture what I would tell my girls if I knew I was about to be arrested and killed.

When Jesus told them about the Holy Spirit, we have to remember he is a gift to us (Acts 2:38), a gift that we can know, for he dwells with us and in us (John 14:17). The Holy Spirit is a gift that Jesus chose to unveil for us in between "I am the way, the truth, and the life" and "I am the true vine." He is a gift that was going to play a huge part of the disciples' lives as they transitioned from having Jesus with them to living life as we do with the Holy Spirit as our helper.

As Jesus started to focus the disciples on the transition that was coming, he stressed two thoughts: "Whatever you ask in my name, I will do it" (John 14:14, 15:16) and "If you love me, you will keep my commandments" (John 14:15, 15:10). As I sat eating lunch with my friend, we were discussing the dynamic of how I want my prayers to be answered but I don't necessarily want to keep the commandments of Christ. This one commandment declares I'm to love others like Jesus loved me (John 15:12). All of the "I am" statements we have studied have led us right up to this step—becoming more focused on others than ourselves. We are not just to be focused, but we are also to love them as much as Jesus loves us.

As a mom I understand and even like what is about to take place. But when I look at myself as the daughter, I don't understand or like it near as much. As you look at the last I am statement, notice what is going to happen.

I am the true vine, and my Father is the vinedresser. Every branch in me that does not bear fruit he takes away, and every branch that does bear fruit he prunes, that it may bear more fruit (John 15:1-2).

Discipline—that's why I said I liked it from a mother's heart because a mother disciplines to bring growth to her children. One of my daughters right now, even though she is already a teenager, is learning to keep a cleaner room. She was blessed to have shared a room with her super-neat older sister, but since we've moved, she has her own room, and cleaning it now falls entirely on her shoulders. Of course, the mess is solely hers also. As we prune this area in her life, I know that as she learns to be neater, it will bring benefits in other areas. But at the same time, when I rightly picture myself as the daughter who will be pruned in this passage, I'm not smiling quite so much.

How do we process Jesus's statement, "Every branch in me that does not bear fruit he takes away"? These people (or branches) are in Jesus, so they would have to be believers—so what is this taken away? Do they die?

The original language gives us a little clue. Literally the word means "to lift up" or "to take away," so it does appear to be death. Dead wood on a vine is worse than being fruitless because dead wood harbors disease and decay. In Acts we read an account of where I believe we see this happening.

But a man named Ananias, with his wife Sapphira, sold a piece of property, and with his wife's knowledge he kept back for himself some of the proceeds and brought only a part of it and laid it at the apostles' feet. But Peter said, "Ananias, why has Satan filled your heart to lie to the Holy Spirit and to keep back for yourself part of the proceeds of the land? While it remained unsold, did it not remain your own? And after it was sold, was it not at your disposal? Why is it that you have contrived this deed in your heart? You have not lied to men but to God." When Ananias heard these words, he fell down and breathed his last. And great fear came upon all who heard of it (Acts 5:1-5).

If, like some try to say, Ananias wasn't saved, then why wouldn't Peter have witnessed to him to bring him to salvation? If he had been an unbeliever, then lying wouldn't have been that horrible, as unbelievers can't be held to a Christian standard. But if we see Ananias as a branch that does not bear fruit being taken away, then all of sudden we are encouraged to open our own eyes and take stock of what kind of vine we are becoming—fruitful or diseased.

But really if you have read this far, I believe you're with me, and we are going through a pruning stage! I pray it is one where we are going to bear more fruit!

As we read through the rest of text, I want us to focus on one thing first. What is Jesus saying will happen? What will we be given?

I am the vine; you are the branches. Whoever abides in me and I in him, he it is that *bears much fruit,* for apart from me you can do nothing. If anyone does not abide in me he is thrown away like a branch and withers; and the branches are gathered, thrown into the fire, and burned. If you abide in me, and my words abide in you, *ask whatever you wish, and it will be done for you.* By this my Father is glorified, that you *bear much fruit* and so prove to be my disciples. As the Father has loved me, so have I loved you. Abide in my love. If you keep my commandments, you will abide in my love, just as I have kept my Father's commandments and abide in his love. These things I have spoken to you, that my *joy may be in you, and that your joy may be full.* "This is my commandment, that you love one another as I have loved you. Greater love has no one than this, that someone lay down his life for his friends. You are my friends if you do what I command you. No longer do I call you servants, for the servant does not know what his master is doing; *but I have called you friends*, for all that I have heard from my Father I have made known to you. You did not choose me, but I chose you and appointed you *that you should go and bear fruit and that your fruit should abide, so that whatever you ask the Father in my name, he may give it to you.* These things I command you, so that you will love one another (John 15:5-17, emphasis added).

These are some pretty fantastic promises: bearing fruit, answered prayers, joy, being called Jesus's friends, and fruit that lasts. I want that, don't you? I know you do; otherwise you would have already closed this book. What kind of fruit do you want to bear? Are you full of joy? When you open your prayer journal, can you look down the list and see prayer after prayer answered? Do you feel like a friend of Jesus?

You already know my answer is no. But just to be brutally honest, the fruit I most desire right now is the fruit of faithfulness because in my heart, I have felt abandoned by God, and that feeling makes me want to walk away. Instead of joy, I have been full of tears. My prayer journal has plenty of requests but few answers. A friend of Jesus? Not so much.

But if we go back to that same passage and underline what we are to do, our eyes may be opened. Go ahead and underline things we are to do.

Abiding. Obedience. Love.

If we start with the abiding, having words of Jesus abiding in our hearts is the key to asking and receiving. Abiding, according to the *Strong's Dictionary*, means to "sojourn" and "to be held, kept, continually." The words of Jesus are held continually in my mind—is that my reality? Is that yours?

What thoughts abide most in my mind? What words do I know by heart? Is it any wonder I was sitting in my garden crying? Is it any wonder the thing I want more than anything is a kind of relationship with Christ that even when my world tilts, my heart stays steadfast? Is it any wonder this kind of relationship is missing?

Thankfully, as we have journeyed together, my heart has changed. As we began, we looked at the four public expressions of "I am":

- • I am the bread of life—a focus on eternal needs versus temporal needs.
- I am the light of the world—a commitment to others still in darkness versus ourselves.
- I am the door of the sheep—Jesus's focus on us and the care he shows us daily.
- I am the good shepherd—Jesus's commitment to us is 100 percent. He will never throw us to the wolves.

If we add the last three, look at the progression we are given.

- I am the resurrection and the life—Jesus's divinity and humanity coming together to give us life both here on earth and in heaven.
- I am the way, the truth, and the life—Jesus is the only way, the only truth, and the only life worth living.
- I am the true vine—Jesus's words abiding in us helps us realize how loved we are. They bring fruit and joy. They call to us as friends talk to friends.

In the beginning, Jesus showed us how to reach out to the world—a world that needs us to focus not on the temporal but on the eternal. This world that needs the light we have been entrusted with. It is hostile to us, but we can walk in daily confidence because our shepherd stands at the door ready as we return from a long day to care for our hurts. He is a shepherd who is always committed to us. We have a very public calling on our lives as believers. Like Peter we say, "Where else would

I go? You have the words to eternal life" (author's paraphrase). As we make that decision with Peter, Jesus invites us into the very personal I am statements.

Jesus's divinity and humanity converge to give us life here and in heaven. But we must be willing to stand on the fact of the only way to God is Jesus, the only truth is Jesus, and the only life is wrapped in Jesus. As we begin to live this life in Jesus, he gives us a precious gift—the Holy Spirit—and a book that we can hold in our hands full of his words. They are words that, when we let them abide in us, will bring fruit, joy, love, and answered prayers.

What are we waiting on? Will we take the knowledge we gained, stand with our brothers and sisters in the book of Acts, and become people who act and who are obedient? Will we become people who know how loved they are so they in turn are able to love others? All you and I have to do is turn the page with a heart ready to act on what we have now been entrusted with: the full expression of who our Jesus is, the I am of God.

The Seven I Am Statements

- I am the bread of life—a focus on eternal needs versus temporal needs.

- I am the light of the world—a commitment to others still in darkness versus ourselves.

- I am the door of the sheep—Jesus's focus on us and the care he shows us daily.

- I am the good shepherd—Jesus's commitment to us is 100 percent. He will never throw us to the wolves.

- I am the resurrection and the life—Jesus's divinity and humanity coming together to give us life both here on earth and in heaven.

- I am the way, the truth, and the life—Jesus is the only way, the only truth, and the only life worth living.

- I am the true vine—Jesus's words abiding in us helps us realize how loved we are. They bring fruit and joy. They call to us as friends talk to friends.

Questions to think about:

Can "pruning" occur as a result of both obedience and disobedience? What is the difference?

Think about a time you were disciplined by the Spirit. What good came out of it? Who benefited from the experience?

If you were to describe yourself to a group of strangers, how would you do it?

Status Quo Challenge: What will you do to focus on others this week?

When was the last time you took a risk,
a real risk?

Devotion

The last of the leaves have recently fallen, transforming from their brilliant shades to a brown, crinkly mess. Some time has gone by since I wrote the first word in this book, and as the seasons have changed, so has my heart. As I have let those seven "I am" statements sink in deep, my thought process has slowly undergone a transformation.

The people in the book of Acts were exactly like us. They had the same kinds of hopes, fears, and troubles. But their lives showed me something my life was missing—the power that enabled them, when difficult days came, to rise to their feet and overcome. They were people who were truly more than conquerors.

> Who shall separate us from the love of Christ? Shall tribulation, or distress, or persecution, or famine, or nakedness, or danger, or sword? As it is written, "For your sake we are being killed all the day long; we are regarded as sheep to be slaughtered." No, in all these things we are more than conquerors through him who loved us. For I am sure that neither death nor life, nor angels nor rulers, nor things present nor things to come, nor powers, nor height nor depth, nor anything else in all creation, will be able to separate us from the love of God in Christ Jesus our Lord. Romans 8:35-39

We can see some of the difficulties people have faced, and still are facing in modern times, which when I put my troubles up against them fade. Really, as I went through the process of letting those seven I am statements change my thinking, I realized how much time and energy I was devoting to issues that are so very temporary.

The book of Acts reminds us we have been given a very important gift—one that will fuel our ability to live our life in a way that will allow others to see and know our God is real. The Holy Spirit is a gift to those who believe—a gift who brings power to a life. Now, since we are believers, we have the same Holy Spirit they did, so why might our lives not be marked by the same power? This power results in answered prayers; it is the power to live in a way that when life turns upside down, we stay steady in our faith.

One thing I'm learning as I study their lives is how focused they were on Christ. He truly was at the center of everything they did. In Acts 2:42-47, we see a picture of this.

They devoted themselves to the apostles' teaching and to the fellowship, to the breaking of bread and the prayers (Acts 2:42).

Do you see the pronoun "they" at the beginning of the sentence? If you're like me, you may be tempted to think it is referring to the apostles, even though it really wouldn't make sense if the apostles were devoted to their own teachings, would it? Somehow, every time I have read this, I pictured in my head the super-Christians. But who is this "they"? In the verse right before, we see who "they" are.

So those who received his word were baptized, and there were added that day about three thousand souls. They devoted themselves to . . . (Acts 2:41-42).

Basically, it is us. I don't consider myself a super-Christian, so I haven't ever thought about how this verse would apply to me. I thought it was just for the preachers, missionaries—you know, people like that. But people like me? Not so much. If I were to write that verse out of the reality of my life, at times it would read like:

They read their Bibles semi-regularly and attend church pretty well, except in the summer—and the winter too, if it's a cold one. Breaking

bread—if that is going out to eat, I can check it off! Prayer, even less
than Bible reading.

Just doesn't seem to have the same punch, does it?

If you asked someone who knows you well if he or she considers
you to be "devoted" to your Bible and church, what would he or
she say? Where it says "breaking of bread," if it is solely referring
to the Lord's Supper, what do we do with that? How does one
become devoted to the Lord's Supper? Possibly it referred to when
believers got together to share a common meal. Their hearts were
so warmed by their love for Christ and each other that an ordinary
meal became an opportunity to show their love to Christ and each
other. Are your meal times like that? Mine aren't.

What about prayer? Do people consider us pray-ers, people
who will really take the time to pray? Better yet, would we
consider ourselves devoted to praying?

How did these people discipline their lives so they were
considered to be devoted? Why is it that in my life, and maybe
yours too, we have somehow got in our minds that these kinds
of experiences are only for the elite, people like Billy Graham?
When in reality they were experienced by the masses in the book
of Acts? Where does that kind of devotion come from?

Awe.

When was the last time you can remember being in awe of
what was happening in the life of the believers you know? When
was the last time you can remember when God was so visibly
at work that the only response you could have was a sense of
awe? That's the reality these people lived. In several places in the
Psalms, we are told to praise God and tell others of his mighty
deeds (Psalm 145:12, 150:2). I can see how, as I have a more
complete understanding of who Jesus said he is, I'm faced with
a choice. Will I invest my heart in him, knowing how completely
we are cared for? Will I trust my day-to-day needs to him and
focus my energies on the eternal needs of others? Making this
change, which seems so simple, has been playing havoc with my
life: my temporal needs verses the eternal needs of others.

Will I—could I—be willing to stop playing my faith so safe, asking only for what seems possible, and exchange that for a faith that is willing to risk everything on the name Jesus?

These people we are about to look at did. They would have had to completely rearrange their lives to be devoted to the teachings, the fellowship, the breaking of bread, and prayer. My husband, Chad, has recently had a spell where deer hunting has taken over our lives. He purchased all kinds of "needed" items to successfully hunt a deer. He spent time in the woods, scouting the perfect place to hunt the deer. He spent time practicing for the moment when he finally would see the deer. There were articles read and re-read, with tips from the experts.

Needless to say, he had to do some rearranging to do all this—all for a something that, in the best case scenario, will feed him for a year. Notice I said feed him; I'm not too sure the rest of us are into eating deer, although he assures me I will like it. But his was a life rearranged for something that in ten years will have little to no significance. Actually, ten years is being optimistic. Come spring, fishing will become his top priority. Seeing him become so devoted to deer hunting has given me a very clear picture of what the believers in the book of Acts would have been doing.

Are we willing to rearrange some things in our lives to become devoted? I think some of us are just desperate enough to be willing to. Maybe we have become so fed up with the status quo in our lives that we crave being able to see God do mighty deeds with our own eyes. As the book of Acts says, "wonders and miraculous signs" were done by the apostles (Acts 2:43) and through the name of "your holy servant Jesus" (Acts 4:30).

Another aspect these believers had in addition to being devoted was they considered themselves as truly being "together and had all things in common."(Acts 2:44) In America, I think for the last decade or two the church and those of us who make up the church have lost this concept. Maybe this is because for so many of us, our needs were met very easily. We had good jobs, credit, rightly or wrongly, was freely available, and for the most part, there was no real need to share. This is not so anymore. As our finances have become tighter and tighter, jobs have been lost, and credit is no longer available (or if it is, we are more cautious of it), we have a new opportunity to make this verse our reality. Could we become people who share?

Something struck me this spring when I was talking with my mom. She said something about how my dad was at a neighbor's house tilling up the ground so they could have a garden. Dad has a tractor; they don't. He shared. It's funny on the flip side, sometimes when someone offers to share with us, we will say no thanks and either try to do it ourselves or give up. I wonder if some of that is just our pride. The people of Acts—the people we want to become like—shared freely with one another. Someone was willing to share, but someone else had to be willing to accept.

As I listen to the news, it doesn't seem as if the economy is going to be changing anytime soon. In fact, as I have watched my grocery bill continue to climb or some weeks stay in price but with fewer bags, I feel confident in saying the next few years we'll find ourselves learning to depend on Christ and each other in new ways.

How can we in our own churches become people who hold everything in common? My mind is thinking through some of the reasons I might not be willing to share. I don't like to share my things if I am honest. One of the top reasons is some people don't take care of things as well as I do. I bet that happened back then too. Another is when I have worked hard for something, I like to know it's mine. That's an ugly sentence, but it's true. Sometimes I don't share what I know because having knowledge gives me an "edge" especially in the working world. At the center of these is a heart who has forgotten that anything I have is there because God gave it to me. The concept of holding "all things in common" (Acts 2:44) strikes a chord in my heart, especially as, in the current economic climate, we may have to become people who depend on each other more and more. The beauty of it is that all the way back in Acts, God's people were doing it and thriving!

As I keep looking at these same six verses, I realize more and more that these people in Acts are far removed from my reality. They were devoted people who saw wonders and miraculous signs—people who shared what they had and then would even sell their possessions to help anyone who had a need. In a group of three thousand plus, how many would have had needs?

In our church, when one of us has a need, especially a financial need from something like sickness or some kind of disaster, our preacher has an old cowboy hat he gets out. He lays the hat on the altar, and anyone who would like to gives. We have seen some mighty giving take place; that hat has overflowed several times, and it is wonderful to see. But what this verse is talking about is a whole different level of giving. It is a level of giving I don't know if I have ever felt where you come home and say, "Their need is more important, so let's sell something to help meet it."

I picture a TV for some reason. I can't imagine coming home from church and selling the TV to help someone. Can you? The absolute closest I can come to identifying with this level of giving is when Chad first lost his job and we were looking at bills and trying to figure out what we could cut. What could we do without in order to pay the bills? As we looked at the list, for some reason the young man we sponsor in Uganda through Compassion International was listed right above the cable bill. We spend $38 a month to help Onesmus have a better life in a faraway land. Our cable bill at the time was close to that. We decided we would not stop sponsoring Onesmus unless we first gave up cable. It was a big step for us and a big commitment. It wasn't a decision we made lightly because we knew we might have to give up cable. That's about as close as I have ever come to being willing to give up a possession to help someone. It's sad but true.

But if we are going to model our lives around these people who knew Jesus—who heard him say "I Am" and came to follow him in the days that ensued—we are going to have to put everything back on the table as a possibility.

Another aspect we see of these people is how, "Day by day, attending the temple together and breaking bread in their homes, they received their food with glad and generous hearts" (Acts 2:46). They came to the temple daily. Can you imagine going to church daily? Back in those days, the temple was open daily, whereas for most of us, our churches are only open a couple of times a week. The principle I see is their eagerness to go. They were excited to walk through the door and worship God; they did not drag themselves to church. If you're like me, when you read this passage, you see them smiling! They had glad and generous hearts. I even imagine they liked the people they went to church with. They were a people devoted.

I'm all about the practical. It's one reason I really have enjoyed studying the seven "I am" statements of Jesus. Through our study, I have been able to see and understand more about who Jesus is and begin to line my life up with what he revealed. This passage is harder for me because I see what I want to be—devoted—but the question is how to accomplish that. I wish there were some kind of checklist we could go through and at the end of it be devoted!

But there's really not a checklist per se but more of a picture painted for us. It is a picture where we can see these people arranging their lives in such a way that Christ became the overwhelming focus of their days. But each of us will have to begin making changes that are personal to us with the goal of Christ becoming our focus.

We have the same resources they had: the teachings of the apostles and the gift of the Holy Spirit. We even have more resources; in addition to our Bibles we have access to a wide range of teaching materials. We have great men and women of the faith who we can pick up a book and read their life story. The challenging part to me, is realizing as I read their life story, their devotion is what made their lives worth imitating. In Acts, we can see these men and women took the same resources we have and began to live their lives in the name of Jesus. They were lives in which we can read miracle after miracle and wonder after wonder in the pages of our Bibles. What I'm lacking, and maybe you are, is the obedience to put it into practice daily.

Living life in the name of Jesus requires more of me than just the knowledge of who he is; I also have to act on it. I must make some decisions and rearrange some areas, all so he becomes the focus of my life. These are hard choices at times as I am becoming a woman devoted to her God, I already know in my heart he's already devoted to me.

Questions to think about:

The risk you took, did you take it out of obedience? What was the result?

What are you devoted to? What does that devotion look like to others?

Has the thought of lowering your standard of living in some way ever occurred to you as a means to share with someone else? Why is this concept hard for many people to accept?

Status Quo Challenge: What will you rearrange in your life this week?

List out your friends, people you spend time with.

Devotion to Prayer

Just seeing the name of Peter is comforting to me. Typically he is someone we identify with easily. He is a fisherman who walked away from his livelihood to follow Jesus—a man who had such faith that he walked on water. Funny, those are not necessarily the parts I identify with. Do you? I find myself identifying more with some of his faults, like talking before thinking, or maybe when he had such a crisis of faith that he denied even knowing Jesus, with a few curse words sprinkled in. (Mark 14:71) But in addition to Peter's failures his devotion stands out. As I let our seven I Am statements play back across my mind, I can see more clearly what Jesus was doing as he revealed them. He was showing us why we should be willing to devote our lives to him.

- *I am the bread of life:* We can focus on eternal needs rather than temporal needs because he's watching over us so closely.
- *I am the light of the world:* We can commit to others who are still in darkness rather than ourselves.
- *I am the door of the sheep:* As we become more and more devoted to him, we become aware of Jesus's focus and care in all kinds of unexpected ways.
- *I am the Good Shepherd:* We can know that he is committed to us 100 percent. We are safe to devote everything into his care.

- *I am the resurrection and the life:* Because of Jesus's divinity and humanity coming together, we will have life both here on earth and in heaven with a Savior who has felt what we feel. We are safe to pour everything in our hearts out to him.
- *I am the way, the truth, and the life:* Jesus is the only way, the only truth, and the only life worth living. This is a clear call to us to devote our lives to him.
- *I am the true vine:* Jesus's words abiding in us help us realize how loved we are. Our devotion will bring fruit and joy.

Any objection we may be tempted to use to stop us from being devoted can be answered with one of the 'I Am' statements. This gives us the freedom to devote ourselves to him or not.

Peter many times is found in the company of John in the Bible. They were a team. If you remember back in Mark 6:7, when Jesus sent out the seventy, they went in pairs, two by two. The early church followed this example, they banded together very tightly so they would have the support they would need to devote their lives to Jesus. We will need the same: friends who share our desire not just to know who Jesus is but to know him in such a way that as life happens all around us, we will find our devotion deepening.

Friends are critical to us. It is only in the last couple of years that I have developed real friendships. For years I had this fear that when people would really get to know me, they would run for the hills! Truthfully, some of my fear was because of a few past failures in friendships. As I started letting down my guard, I can vividly remember having a conversation with a friend named Connie. She is one of the friendliest people you will ever meet. She also has a huge heart and makes you feel loved in a matter of minutes. I was driving home from work and talking to her, and all of sudden I blurted out, "There is a good chance if we keep talking, in few weeks you'll realize you don't really like me." It was a very awkward moment in the conversation to say the least. As the months and years have gone on, my fears have never materialized. Instead, our friendship has grown. The friendships we develop are great opportunities for ministry to happen where people can be impacted in ways that change their lives forever—not with a whole lot of fanfare but just during the normal course of life. Connie has spoken encouragement into my life many days, and I hope I have hers too.

The early Christians in their devotion prayed for signs and wonders to accompany their ministries (Acts 4:29-30). When I say ministries, I'm not talking only about the apostles but the regular people in the church who began to serve in all kinds of ways. Stephen comes to mind as one of my favorites, maybe because of how we see him serving. I get to see people serve regularly in much the same way he did.

In the early church, some of the widows were being overlooked in the food distribution, and a complaint was made. I don't think they were being overlooked on purpose, but with the kind of growth the early church was experiencing, problems were sure to arise. Regardless of why they were overlooked, we get a glimpse showing us how churches will never be perfect because they are made up of humans. This church had all of the apostles in attendance, well with the exception of Judas. But by this point he had been replaced with a man named Mathhias(Acts 1:26), and people still got hurt in the church. But when this complaint was made, the twelve summoned the full number of disciples. Can you imagine the group that gathered? The apostles knew they couldn't do everything. They had to focus on what they had been called to do, but at the same time, they had to look at the problem and deal with it. They knew they needed help distributing the food. Look at the criteria they used to find these people to serve:

Therefore, brothers, pick out from among you seven men of good repute, full of the Spirit and of wisdom, whom we will appoint to this duty (Acts 6:3).

It's critical that we keep in mind what these seven men were going to be doing: handing out food to widows. I love imaging this scene because at our food pantry, I see the faces of the people who work week after week handing out food to those in need. These are people who have much in common with Stephen. The point I'm trying to make is these seven people were people, just as you and I are. They had a good reputation and were full of the Spirit and of wisdom. They were willing to serve because they were devoted to Jesus.

Stephen, I feel confident, would have been one of those in attendance back when the believers gathered together to pray for God's protection and boldness in their lives. It was a boldness that included asking God to "stretch out your hand to heal, and signs and wonders are performed through the name of your holy servant Jesus" (Acts 4:30). It's easy, when we see a verse like this, to apply it only to apostles back in those days. But that's not what happens. Stephen, a normal man who had become a believer and devoted his life to Jesus, was one of those who saw God do exactly what he had asked for.

And Stephen, full of grace and power, was doing great wonders and signs among the people (Acts 6:8)

What kinds of wonders and signs do you suppose Stephen did in the course of handing out food to those widows many would have been tempted to overlook? Did he look in their eyes and offer them hope that their God saw them in their loneliness? Did he pray that what food he gave them would last? We don't know everything Stephen did, but we know it was full of grace and power. A devoted life will show itself in care for others in a million ways. Those of us in Christ have been gifted with a way to impact others, but it's when our own individual hearts become devoted to Jesus that our gifts will burst into a flame!

Peter and John, like Stephen, did exploits that many of us are tempted to shake our heads and think happened only in times past or only to the special ones. But it's not that some are special and the rest of us are not; it's all about whether we will take the time to discover who Jesus is and let him grab our heart. Then devotion will come. It's easier to become devoted to someone when you know how much he or she cares for you.

One of the exploits Peter and John did is recorded in Acts 3:1-10. As you look at these verses, notice what Peter and John were doing:

Now Peter and John were going up to the temple at the hour of prayer, the ninth hour. And a man lame from birth was being carried, whom they laid daily at the gate of the temple that is called the Beautiful Gate to ask alms of those entering the temple. Seeing Peter and John about to go into the temple, he asked to receive alms. And Peter directed his gaze at him, as did John, and said, "Look at us." And he fixed his attention on them, expecting to receive something from them. But Peter said, "I have no silver and gold, but what I do have I give to you. In the name of Jesus Christ of Nazareth, rise up and walk!" And he took him by the right hand and raised him up, and immediately his feet and ankles were made strong. And leaping up he stood and began to walk, and entered the temple with them, walking and leaping and praising God. And all the people saw him walking and praising God, and recognized him as the one who sat at the Beautiful Gate of the temple, asking for alms. And they were filled with wonder and amazement at what had happened to him.

One of the things I have noticed in the book of Acts is how devoted they were to prayer. It intrigued me when I read that they were praying at "the hour of prayer." When I did a little research[6] I found that fixed-hour prayer had its origins in Judaism. They had certain times of the day when they stopped and prayed. Sometimes they went and prayed with a group and sometimes alone. In the back of the book, I have listed a resource I consulted on fixed prayers if it intrigues you also.

We can see some of the examples of fixed praying in the Old Testament. One example would be Daniel: "He got down on his knees three times a day and prayed and gave thanks before his God" (Daniel 6:10). The Jewish people still pray three times daily. Peter and John were heading to the temple to pray at three o'clock in the afternoon when they encountered the lame man. A miracle is about to occur, but I suppose as they were walking they had no idea what God was about to do.

To give you a little background of the land they were living in during this time period, the Roman Empire had very distinct ways of organizing the day. A bell rang at six o'clock in the morning to start the day, and throughout the day, the bell rang to mark the day's progress, all the way up until six o'clock, marking the end of the market day. I thought about Peter and John heading to the temple to pray. They would have done this every day according to custom. As I thought about this, I realized how many practices they put into place to help them to focus on their devotion. It wasn't just a ritual. The relationship they had with Christ made it a rich time of being together.

This made me think back to when Chad was in the army, and we would have set times to call one another. There is no way I would have missed it! This was before the days of cell phones, email, or Skype, so I was willing to rearrange my day to make those phone calls happen. I've been trying to put some of this fixed-hour praying into my schedule, and it's helping. Notice I said "some." The practice as it is can be pretty structured, so I'm taking the parts that work for me personally and leaving the rest. However, just knowing that I have a set time where I'm planning on praying has made my prayer time more consistent.

The next portion I noticed in the story is when Peter says, "I have no silver and gold, but what I do have I give to you. In the name of Jesus Christ of Nazareth, rise up and walk!" Peter may not have had silver and gold, but he had a belief in power in the name of Jesus. I mentioned in the very first pages how these people lived life in the name of Jesus in a way that I want to.

What does it mean to do something in the name of Jesus? When we are living a life where we are surrendered to Jesus—where his words are abiding in us—we will start to feel a compulsion to do something. I believe we will start to be in situations where we are going to need to know how to use the name of Jesus in the way the early church did. It didn't just mean to them that they were doing it in remembrance of Jesus. When they used that expression, "in the name of Jesus," they were expressing the very nature of his being. When they used this phrase, they were inviting the Holy Spirit to be present and available in the exact situation.

Peter was not just asking Jesus to heal the man but pronouncing Jesus over the crippled beggar, thereby revealing the power of Jesus in that situation. How would that look in our lives?

It's going to depend on how God has gifted us, our boldness will come when we surrender our own lives and choose to devote them to Jesus. When we do that, we will become confident enough to pray with boldness and power, knowing that the power is coming through the name of Jesus. Like with Stephen, we don't know exactly what miracles were taking place as he served food, we just know they happened.

I had heard that phrase for so long—and it had just become something we closed our prayers with—it really didn't hold much meaning at all to me on a practical level. I considered it to have some sentimental value but practically, no real power.

That is until now. I am starting to see that when we start operating our lives in this power, we will see the wonders with our eyes. I found a quote[7] from a theologian named Thomas Aquinas (1225-1274) that sums up so much of what I have felt and have even seen on some levels:

Thomas Aquinas once called on Pope Innocent II when he was counting out a large sum of money. The Pope remarked, "You see, Thomas, the church can no longer say, 'silver and gold have I none.'" Aquinas replied, "True holy father, but neither can she now say, 'Rise and walk.'"

Very telling, don't you think?

We could continue looking at the lives of the people of the book of Acts, but we would find the same picture over and over.

A life devoted becomes one full of grace and power. We have looked at the power aspect, but what does it mean to be full of grace?

Grace is *charis* in the Greek[8] —the favor of God. The unmerited favor of God; sounds wonderful, right? Months ago as I sat in the garden, I had wanted the favor of God to show up in a way where money would become available, quickly and abundantly. It hadn't, and tears fell. My heart felt like God had held out on me. Maybe I wasn't good enough, maybe I wasn't trying hard enough, maybe Chad had some hidden sin in his life—my mind brought up all kinds of reasons for why I wasn't seeing the favor of God. I really wanted to know why wasn't I experiencing the favor of God, and those questions drove me to ask God, "Why?"

As the months have worn on and I started letting those 'I Am' statements shape my thinking instead of what the culture says, my heart started changing. They are small baby steps, but they are change. I started having this desire to devote my life to Jesus instead of a life devoted to Jenny. My reality hasn't changed. Christmas this year is going to be tight—more than likely the smallest Christmas our family has had—but it's different. I'm not crying. I don't feel abandoned. I know that Jesus is watching over us and making sure we will have what we need to celebrate his birth. He is the Good Shepherd.

I recently saw this play out in a very personal way. Writing is a very solitary activity. There are five of us in our house, and some of the five many times have friends over. We have a pretty standard house but one that doesn't have any extra rooms, like an office or a separate dining room, so most times you would find me writing in the living room on the couch. This was a real struggle at times; actually, a struggle most times.

The other morning, I had gotten up early—and I mean early—to write, and I was praying, just asking that I could have some time alone to write. Then my heart started doing that thing where we start saying, "If only I had a house with my very own office or a big bedroom where I could have a corner all to myself." All of a sudden our utility room flashed across my mind.

Now our utility room is not a room I go into often. In fact, I would estimate I was in it about four times in the last year. It's tiny, dark—mainly because no one has put a light bulb in it—and full of junk that didn't get unpacked.

As I sat there, though, I felt like God had planted the idea in my head. I walked out into the room and noticed it was bigger than I remembered. It had a couple of electrical sockets and two shelves across the wall. All of a sudden, it hit me: this could be my very own writing space! I cleaned it out in matter of hours, and considering cleaning out rooms is not high on my list, you know it was that burst of energy you get when you are excited! I painted it my favorite color—teal—and went and bought some bright-patterned carpet squares, which Chad installed. He also put the light bulb in. For less than seventy dollars, I now have the space I needed, all because I was in a place where I felt safe pouring out my heart to Jesus, and he could direct me. He is the Good Shepherd.

The favor of God—we want it, but we want it to happen without the relationship and obedience on our part. We also are prone to want exactly what I wanted as I sat in the garden and cried: for our very temporal needs to be met. In the book of Acts, we see Stephen, who was said to be "full of grace and power," full of the favor of God, and yet a few pages over, we find Stephen being stoned to death and Peter and John arrested and beaten—yet they are our example of life being lived in the name of Jesus. Their lives reflected an eternal view where we are still benefiting from them.

As we have taken this journey together, at some point the dots have connected in my heart, and I hope in yours too. Jesus shared who he is with us so our hearts would become devoted to him. When that happens, it doesn't matter so much what happens because our most dear possession—our relationship with Jesus—can never be taken away from us. Everything else starts to dim in comparison.

We begin to care more about what Jesus is doing in the world than what the world is doing to us. At the same time, though, we have been given some rights and authority, which we are supposed to know and operate in as we live life in his name. We'll spend the next pages exploring those so we can start to fully grasp how we make the change from simply living life to living life in the name of Jesus. It is a life I pray will find us both, full of grace and power.

Questions to think about:

Look back at your list of friends. Are they people you pray with? If not, why not?

When you look at your average day, do you see a pattern? Is your day arranged around certain activities? What are they?

When you hear the words "filled with grace and power", what image from today's world comes to mind?

Status Quo Challenge: How will you plan your day to pray differently this week?

Have you ever felt like your rights had been violated? Describe the situation.

CHAPTER 9

Rights

Rights and authority—that doesn't quite sound like something we are suppose to be talking about, does it? In fact, your mind might be like mine, and you might have thought, *Aren't we called to give up our rights?* It's strange to me how I reacted to the words "exercising our rights and authority." It took me a couple of days to realize what exactly was going on. As we have learned more about Jesus and then have seen the early church act on their knowledge with devotion, we are coming face to face with a decision. If we devote ourselves to Christ, we will be involved in a conflict. The conflict starts in our own hearts. We have to make our flesh line up with the Scriptures. We have to begin to see ourselves as Christ does. Or we won't ever see the power and feel the security that comes when we are living life in the name of Christ. I pray that as you have journeyed with me your own battle is being waged and won. I started to feel the security in my life when the truth finally made it in to those deep places in my heart.

Christmas was only a couple of days ago, and I shared with you how we knew it was going to be tough. In addition to the financial stress, we had the normal family tensions over extended schedules, and all the other stresses of the Christmas season. Normally, I find myself at one of two extremes-crying or in a rage. This year, though, was different. Even though the family didn't change and we didn't inherit a windfall, I knew Jesus was watching me closely as I walked out into the world every day. He knew my feelings would get hurt. He knew I would be walking around the mall with a firm budget and a list for the girls' gifts, trying to make them match. Knowing he's the Good Shepherd caused me to be able to not let those things fester but to bring them to him and let him tend them quickly. On Christmas night, Chad and I said this was the best Christmas we have had in a long time—a very long time. The only real difference was my heart. I'm beginning to see how winning this conflict has a very real impact on my daily life. In ways I could have never anticipated.

If we had to stop right here, I believe we would be able to live out the rest of our lives with a new sense of security that isn't going to ebb and flow but stay steady. However, the early church took the security they had in Christ and let the Holy Spirit flow through them in such a way that every generation since has looked at the book of Acts and noticed the power of those people's lives.

They exercised the rights they had in Christ daily and began to use the authority he had given them to reach out and touch the lives of people all around them. So why did my mind react so strongly to even start thinking about our rights and authority in Christ?

The conflict—begins in our hearts but moves to a whole different level when we start living life in the name of Jesus. Our enemy knows he will be affected. Satan knows when believers win the conflict in their own hearts, their lives will become devoted to Jesus. Satan realizes he has a man or woman who God will start to trust with his power, just like he did with the believers in Acts.

I went and looked at the Scriptures where we are taught to lay down our rights and I realized it doesn't apply to the rights we have been given **in** Christ. As you look at the next verses, pay special attention to what kind of rights we are called to lay down.

> Do nothing from selfish ambition or conceit, but in humility count others more significant than yourselves. Let each of you look not only to his own interests, but also to the interests of

others. Have this mind among yourselves, which is yours in Christ Jesus, who, though he was in the form of God, did not count equality with God a thing to be grasped, but emptied himself, taking the form of a servant, being born in the likeness of men. And being found in human form, he humbled himself by becoming obedient to the point of death, even death on a cross. Therefore God has highly exalted him and bestowed on him the name that is above every name, so that at the name of Jesus every knee should bow, in heaven and on earth and under the earth, and every tongue confess that Jesus Christ is Lord, to the glory of God the Father (Philippians 2:3-11).

We lay down our rights to a selfish and vain life so we can care for others. Jesus has been given a name that is above every other name, and that's the name we are to operate our lives out of. A name that will cause every knee to bow and every tongue to confess Jesus as Lord, can you imagine the sight?

In the New International Version (NIV) we can see this word "rights":

But when the time had fully come, God sent his Son, born of a woman, born under law, to redeem those under law, that we might receive the full rights of sons. Because you are sons, God sent the Spirit of his Son into our hearts, the Spirit who calls out, "Abba, Father" (Galatians 4:4-6 NIV).

In the English Standard Version (ESV), instead of rights it says, "We might receive adoption as sons." Basically, whichever wording you use, we have been adopted into the family of God. Before we get into what some of those rights are. Have you ever thought about what it means to be part of the family of God? Sometimes things come up in my family, and we tell our girls, "Listen we just don't do that because of who we are." One thing that I am prone to tell my girls a lot is, "The Bible is the inspired Word of God, and as such we treat it with respect." It's just part of what I would call our family legacy—things that I pray are passed from generation to generation. Another one I often tell them is, "Every choice brings life or death to you on some level."

What do you think Jesus would tell us?

We don't even have to guess really. We saw in Philippians that we should count others as more significant than ourselves. Can you picture hearing Jesus say, "I'm so glad you're part of my family, but you have to know we count others as more significant than ourselves. We serve people." Can you image what would happen in our families, towns, and states if enough of us let this be part of who we are? Did you have bad service at a restaurant? The waitress is more significant than your dining experience.

We keep going around the same circle: a focus not on our temporal needs but an eye toward the eternal plan of God and our part in it. Our rights as part of the family of God aren't going to be focused entirely on what we get but what we are able to do. Over the holidays, I saw Princess Kate on the news, and she was talking to kids who were standing outside waiting for a chance to see the princess. She has been given access to all kinds of places and opportunities that most of us will never see, but as a princess, she is expected to act a certain way. A good princess always has a gracious word on her lips, she is always dressed wonderfully, and she uses her influence and power to champion the cause of the poor and needy. We are called to these same three principles as sons and daughters of the King:

- "Let your speech always be gracious, seasoned with salt, so that you may know how you ought to answer each person" (Colossians 4:6).
- "Put on then, as God's chosen ones, holy and beloved, compassionate hearts, kindness, humility, meekness, and patience, bearing with one another and, if one has a complaint against another, forgiving each other; as the Lord has forgiven you, so you also must forgive.

And above all these put on love, which binds everything together in perfect harmony" (Colossians 3:12-14).

- "And let our people learn to devote themselves to good works, so as to help cases of urgent need, and not be unfruitful" (Titus 3:14).

I'm not sure I start my day out as I'm sure Kate Middleton does, fully aware that as a princess the whole world is watching to see what she does and says. Do you? Would it change us if we started out thinking each morning that as we interact with people, we are part of the royal family of God? Can you even imagine how much air time it would get on CNN if Princess Kate acted as some of us have in public?

When I said Princess Kate had access to places and opportunities most of us never will have, my mind immediately thought of what we have been given access to that most people will never have access to: God. I think for our generations we have are losing a sense of what a privilege this access to God is. We may have had it in previous generations, but it seems to be disappearing from ours. Really nowadays we have access on some level to everybody. Even presidents have Twitter accounts, and use them. But imagine what it must have been like for the people who had gone to the temple time after time to present their sacrifices to a priest, who would in turn go to another part of the temple and present the person's sacrifice. If you weren't a priest, you never would be able to go into the part of the temple where the very presence of God was. Never, no matter how desperate your prayer was.

My mind wandered back through the pages of Scripture and settled in on the story of Hannah when she was so distressed and prayed to the Lord, weeping bitterly. As she sat there pouring her heart out, the priest observed her and said, "How long will you go on being drunk? Put your wine away from you" (1 Samuel 1:14). Can you imagine? All those generations, there's this distance from God, because of sin, but the priest was as close as most could get to interacting with God. And in Hannah's case the priest thought she was drunk! The greatest right and privilege we have been given through Jesus is the right of access to God.

> For we do not have a high priest who is unable to sympathize with our weaknesses, but one who in every respect has been tempted as we are, yet without sin. Let us then with confidence draw near to the throne of grace, that we may receive mercy and find grace to help in time of need (Hebrews 4:15-16).

> And because you are sons, God has sent the Spirit of his Son into our hearts, crying, "Abba, Father!" (Galatians 4:6).

As Hannah poured out her heart, do you know what she would have thought if she had been able to go directly to the throne of grace for help instead of going to the temple to sit in the presence of one who would judge her to be drunk? Are we exercising this right?

In Acts, we see people come confidently to the throne of grace to receive mercy and find grace to help them in their needs because they know Jesus stands there as not only their Savior but as their co-heir (Galatians 4:7) They exercised this right, I believe, with a reverence we don't have because we have taken it for granted. Somehow our generation has taken the motto, "People are just people" and applied it to God. It's causing us to lose some of our wonder at what we have been given as children of God. But if we sit back and let our minds think through the privilege we have been given, would it change our hearts when we are in need?

All the times I have found myself like Hannah crying in my garden or at my kitchen sink, did I realize what a gift I have been given to have the right to go to God and pour out my heart as a daughter to her father? We aren't able to exercise our authority in Christ until we start realizing the rights we have been given and conduct ourselves as such.

What do you see as the difference between "rights" and "authority"?

When in Galatians it says we "might receive the full rights as sons," the rights it is talking about having is "the nature and condition of the true disciples in Christ, who by receiving the Spirit of God into their souls become sons of God," according to *Strong's Dictionary*.[9] The rights we have been given are ours because we have been adopted into the family of God through Christ. We don't have to do anything; we have already been given these rights. One of them would be our ability to approach the throne of grace in times of trouble. Another is being able to call out to God as "Abba." This right that believers have only through Jesus marks us in a way which will be obvious to others.

The people of the book of Acts lived lives that were marked. People recognized them as different because they carried themselves as people who knew who they were sons and daughters of God.

I so want to carry myself like that: a woman who speaks graciously, clothed with love, and devoted first to Christ and then to good works. As I have been learning to carry myself rightly I have found myself at the throne of grace, looking for help and mercy more and more. The world is too desperate for us not to come across people who need help. The other morning I received an email from a friend in need, and as I approached God's throne, I did so with an awareness of the great right and privilege it is. I also found myself in need of mercy as I struggle against my own sinful nature many days.

My heart has become much more secure in the months from when I wrote the first page in this book to now. My life has taken on more devotion as I have walked this out over the course of these last several months. I realize all I have been given is in part so I'll be able to start exercising the authority Christ has given us who believe. It is an authority that isn't meant to be lorded over someone else but an authority to respond just as Jesus would.

We saw that in Acts 3, when Peter said to the lame beggar, "In the name of Jesus Christ of Nazareth, rise up and walk." He exercised the authority he had, and the man walked. Amazing!

My biggest concern when I first started this book was what would I do with all the miracles of Acts. How would I explain them since they seem to be so rare in my sphere of life? What I didn't know when I started this journey was that as I have followed the Scriptures, something became very apparent to me: devotion.

Could it be the reason we see so few miracles is we are so little devoted to Jesus? We have such a small amount of knowledge of him, our lives are arranged around our own interests, and we approach prayer not as a right and privilege but as a chore so that we aren't even in touch with what Jesus would do through us, if he had our devotion.

I think that is true for me.

I don't know how long it takes for us to get a place where we can be entrusted with the power we see in the book of Acts, but I know it will be a life that's marked by obedience and devotion. We could start studying the authority we have in Christ, but I'm not ready for it. I'm still sifting, soaking, and changing to become a woman whose knowledge of who Jesus said he is gives her security deep down. I am becoming a woman whose security, causes her to stand up and carry herself in a way that reflects who she is: a daughter of the King who is exercising her right to call God "Abba" and pray to him right at the throne of grace.

I think when I have made this portion part of who I am, and allow it to sink all the way down into my marrow, then I'll be ready to learn what authority I have in Christ. But right now, I would simply be adding knowledge I'm not ready to live out yet.

Maybe, like me, you're making some changes. Changes take time to become permanently part of who we are. I've read many a book where I learned so much that I didn't seem to know what to apply. As I have worked on these principles over the course of a year, coming face to face with my priorities as opposed to what Jesus says my priority should be, has been life altering. Devotion takes time to develop, and I hope you'll give your heart time to develop too.

Jesus showed us through the seven "I Am" statements what life was all about, and then the people of Acts showed us how knowing this truth is what causes a life to be secure, regardless of what is going on around us. The Holy Spirit, who is a gift to us, empowers us to reach out to a world that desperately needs Jesus. But we haven't seen much of God. Oh I know that as the Trinity, they are all there. But I mean in a way where we see God individually in this journey. He's there. In fact, if it's possible, I think the next chapter of this book will bring all this together in a way that will thrill your heart at how meticulous God is in his plans for us.

Questions to think about:

After reading this chapter, do you still feel as though you had been wronged?

What are your rights as a member of Christ's family? Do you feel comfortable in exercising them?

What would exercising your rights and authority in Christ look like? How would it be perceived in today's world?

Status Quo Challenge: How will you approach the throne of mercy and grace differently this week?

When you speak with God,
what do you call him? Why?

CHAPTER 10

The Great I AM

We are stepping back deep into the Old Testament—all the way back to Exodus. Moses was keeping the flock of his father-in-law and going about his day-to-day life when he experienced God. Moses's encounter changed not only the course of Moses's life but countless others. That's what I pray is beginning to happen in our own lives: a radical change in our hearts where our lives become strong in the Lord. I pray we have lives where, when the world tilts, we remain steadfast. We already know in our lifetimes that the world will shake. It has from generation to generation, but I believe we now will be armed to stand steady, living our lives in the name of Jesus.

Now Moses was keeping the flock of his father-in-law, Jethro, the priest of Midian, and he led his flock to the west side of the wilderness and came to Horeb, the mountain of God. And the angel of the LORD appeared to him in a flame of fire out of the midst of a bush. He looked, and behold, the bush was burning, yet it was not consumed. And Moses said, "I will turn aside to see this great sight, why the bush is not burned." When the LORD saw that he turned aside to see, God called to him out of the bush, "Moses, Moses!" And he said, "Here I am." Then he said, "Do not come near; take your sandals off your feet, for the place on which you are standing is holy ground." And he said, "I am the God of your father, the God of Abraham, the God of Isaac, and the God of Jacob." And Moses hid his face, for he was afraid to look at God. Then the LORD said, "I have surely seen the affliction of my people who are in Egypt and have heard their cry because of their taskmasters. I know their sufferings, and I have come down to deliver them out of the hand of the Egyptians and to bring them up out of that land to a good and broad land, a land flowing with milk and honey, to the place of the Canaanites, the Hittites, the Amorites, the Perizzites, the Hivites, and the Jebusites. And now, behold, the cry of the people of Israel has come to me, and I have also seen the oppression with which the Egyptians oppress them. Come, I will send you to Pharaoh that you may bring my people, the children of Israel, out of Egypt." But Moses said to God, "Who am I that I should go to Pharaoh and bring the children of Israel out of Egypt?" (Exodus 3:1-11).

Can you imagine how Moses felt as he stood there? Maybe he felt guilty because he had been spared from a life of slavery. Maybe the sights and smells came back to him from when he ventured down to see his people (Exodus 2). Whatever Moses felt, we can read exactly what God felt: compassion. God had seen his people and heard their cries. Knowing that God sees me and hears my cries brings a certain amount of comfort but nothing like knowing that at some point God will move on the behalf of his people—me and you!

[God] said, "But I will be with you, and this shall be the sign for you, that I have sent you: when you have brought the people out of Egypt, you shall serve God on this mountain." Then Moses said to God, "If I come to the people of Israel and say to them, 'The God of your fathers has sent me to you,' and they ask me, 'What is his name?' what shall I say to them?" (Exodus 3:12-13).

This always brings a smile to my face. Look at the sign Moses was given. When Moses completed the mission—bringing the people out of Egypt—then he would serve God and know he had been sent. That is not the kind of confirmation I want. What about you? I prefer a sign that will confirm the plan of God right up front. Do you think that sometimes we miss God's plan because we are waiting for the sign before we step out?

> God said to Moses, "I AM WHO I AM." And he said, "Say this to the people of Israel, 'I AM has sent me to you.'" God also said to Moses, "Say this to the people of Israel, 'The LORD, the God of your fathers, the God of Abraham, the God of Isaac, and the God of Jacob, has sent me to you.' This is my name forever, and thus I am to be remembered throughout all generations (Exodus 3:14-15).

Here we see God introduce himself as the "I AM"—the name of God that is to be remembered throughout all generations. Do you see in the verse above where it says "LORD" in all capital letters? If we were looking at the Hebrew, it would say "YHWH," which is the personal name of God. The word Jehovah originated from an attempt to pronounce the consonants YHWH with the vowels from the word Adonai, another name of God that means Lord. In the oldest Hebrew texts, there are no vowels. That's a bit confusing, isn't it?

Let me boil it down to how my head has processed it. I AM, Yahweh, and Jehovah all come from this same root passage, and in our English Bibles, the way we see it is as LORD. It is the most common usage of a name of God in the Old Testament. According to John Piper[10], it occurs 6,828 times. Unfortunately, we miss the beauty of it because LORD sounds just like a title. It even has a little bit of a negative connotation in our minds. In actuality, God was inviting Moses into a personal relationship where Moses knew him on a first-name basis. It's pretty awesome when you think about being invited into a personal relationship with God where you're able to call him by his first name.

As the years went on from here, the Jewish people regarded this as the most holy name of God, and they wouldn't even speak it. They were trying so hard to follow the Ten Commandments, and as they started adding rules, someone decided it was too risky to say God's name. Fear of breaking the commandment of taking name of the "LORD your God" in vain was at the heart of the practice (see Deuteronomy 5:11). Unfortunately, today no one knows what it sounded like. This personal name—the proper name of God—shows us that God has always desired to be on a first-name basis with us.

One thought nagged me the first time I studied this thoroughly: if LORD is introduced in Exodus 3, why can we see it in Genesis? Just in case that occurred to you also, this is because scholars believe Moses wrote Genesis sometime after the Exodus. When I read in the Old Testament and see LORD I try to stop and pay just a bit closer attention because its meaning is personal, to those on a first-name basis with God. Interestingly, the very first time you see LORD is in Genesis 2:4, right when mankind is created.

When God said he was the I AM, he was basically telling us he is everything we need. In the Old Testament, God was invisible. People knew of him, heard his voice, and saw the power of God, but they couldn't reach out and touch him. Because of his holiness and our sinfulness, we would have dropped dead if we had saw or touched him. When Jesus came, it provided us with a bridge that could span the gulf created by sin.

Colossians 1:15 tells us that Jesus is "the image of the invisible God." Jesus came so we could see God. Every time Jesus shared one of those I Am statements, he was inviting us into a closer relationship with God. He was showing us the very personal side of God—how he cares for us and how he wants us to be the light. When you think of what Moses was to do—which was to be the human representative to go and set the slaves or captives free—we see how we are very much called to do the same thing.

We see that Jesus very clearly identified himself as the I Am in John 8:58-59.

> Jesus said to them, "Truly, truly, I say to you, before Abraham was, I am." So they picked up stones to throw at him, but Jesus hid himself and went out of the temple.

The beauty of our invitation to know Jesus through the I Am statements is that they really are an invitation to understand the personality of God. Jesus came to show us God. Too many Christians have this view of God where we see Jesus as the "nice" side and God as the "angry" side. In reality, however, Jesus is the exact image of God. They are identical twins, you might say. The people who picked up the stones to kill Jesus were doing it because they believed he was committing blasphemy by taking on the most revered name of God. It was one they wouldn't even speak. Do you imagine that when the people decided to separate themselves from God by not speaking his name because of their fear that his heart was grieved? Don't forget that when God told the name to Moses, it was to be God's name "forever" and to be "remembered throughout all generations" (Exodus 3:15). I believe God was grieved. I imagine that God smiled when Jesus stood up and said:

- I am the Bread of Life
- I am the Light of the World
- I am the Gate for the sheep
- I am the Good Shepherd
- I am the Resurrection and the Life
- I am the Way, and the Truth, and the Life
- I am the True Vine

All the power of God, all the care of God, and everything our hearts need, Jesus is and God is. He is the great I Am. It is a mystery our hearts may never understand until we see it with our own eyes but a mystery where we can rest secure in the care of God, who wants us to know him personally.

We have one more place to visit before begin to part ways—not forever, I hope, but just for a time. I hope both our hearts soak in this knowledge and live it out in our corners of life.

We find Jesus's last use of I Am at his arrest. It was a moment where once again I believe we can see the humanity and divinity of Jesus come face to face with people. The outcome was much different than when we saw it before with Mary at the death of Lazarus when Jesus wept with her. In that case, we saw the humanity of Jesus on display as his heart was moved. This time his divinity will take center stage.

A band of soldiers have come with officers to arrest Jesus. As they are walking, do you think their minds wondered why it was going to take so many of them to arrest a teacher? It's interesting to see what they brought with them.

> So Judas, having procured a band of soldiers and some officers from the chief priests and the Pharisees, went there with lanterns and torches and weapons (John 18:3).

We don't know how many soldiers came, but we know they came armed. Some scholars put the number as high as a thousand men. Can you imagine the scene as a group of armed soldiers made their way to arrest Jesus—a carpenter and a teacher—with his followers—fishermen, tax collectors, common men?

I imagine some of them must have thought it was a waste of their time and energy to bring so many men out to arrest such an easy target. At the same, I wonder if maybe the chief priest knew anyone who could do all the miracles Jesus did might just be a bit hard to capture. In several places we see them on the verge of either trying to take him or stone him but he was able to elude them (John 8:59, 12:36). Maybe the priest had an inkling of what could have happened.

Our Jesus walked forward, knowing that the time had come for him to "lay down his life" so he could take it up again (John 10:17). He asked them a simple question: "Whom do you seek?" (John 18:4)

They answered him, "Jesus of Nazareth." Jesus said to them, "I am he" (John 18:5a).

Different versions of the Bible handle this text differently. Above is the English Standard Version, but in some of the other versions, it will look something like, "I am *he*," or it might have brackets around it. What they are trying to show is the "he" really isn't there in the original language. It was added for ease of reading. I'm going to rewrite it, leaving out the "he."

They answered him, "Jesus of Nazareth." Jesus said to them, "I am." Judas, who betrayed him, was standing with them. When Jesus said to them, "I am," they drew back and fell to the ground (John 18:5-6).

A band of soldiers heard Jesus say, "I am," and they fell to their knees. Maybe like me, your mind is thinking of the verse that says, "At the name of Jesus every knee should bow" (Philippians 2:10). Jesus is facing the hardest days of his life, and all that power—all his divinity—meets and pours out of his mouth with two little words, and they fall to their knees.

As we have studied these I Am statements, I hope your heart has been affected. They show us who God is. They give us an insight into his personality so we can begin to live our lives in the power of the name of Jesus. Can you imagine at some point being able to actually say this name of God in heaven? He shared a name with us that we lost the ability to say, but through Jesus, we can know what it means and look forward to the day when we are able to say it.

Living life in the name of Jesus has taken on a whole new dimension, hasn't it?

Questions to think about:

How do our habits impact our relationship with I Am?

Has God ever spoken to you? How did you respond?

Why do you suppose it is difficult for most people to see God as the Great I Am?

Status Quo Challenge: What will you do this week to learn about who God really is?

Take some time and write out your personal testimony. Try to keep it down to 6-8 sentences.

A Sure Foundation

Yesterday I had the opportunity to share a few thoughts at a kids' basketball game during halftime. Most of people were strangers to me, and it's rather intimidating to walk out and share something that is supposed to help them to look afresh at Jesus in six minutes or less—especially with a big clock counting down and knowing it will buzz loudly if you go over!

I thought of you as I walked onto the court. I love to write for people who know me, but it's much more intimidating when I let my mind wander down the path of who will eventually pick this book up to read. What will be going on in their lives when they sit down to read it? Will they—you, in fact—be inspired to look afresh at Jesus? Thankfully, I have had more than six minutes during this journey.

When I started this journey, I was smack-dab in the middle of a very hard season. Now, almost a year later, so many of the circumstances that were causing my heart to tremble remain a part of my life. The situation I mentioned where I cried at the sink is still going on. Prices still seem to be on a rollercoaster. The only difference is *my* heart.

As I walked onto the basketball court, I looked in those faces and imagined you. Maybe it was because they were strangers that I could put their faces to yours, but I shared exactly what I would if you and I were sitting in my living room and we had only a few minutes together. Our time during that particular day would have been very short because Meghan, my oldest daughter, was heading back to college. I hate when she leaves. I had told Chad the night before that I love when I lay down at night and know all of my family is safe and sound under our roof.

I shared with those in attendance how I had gotten gas the night before, and I was shocked by how much gas had gone up since I had last filled up. I know, like many of you, that when we spend more on gas, we spend less somewhere else. I was so thankful when my mind immediately went to how Jesus is the Good Shepherd. I have no idea what the next years hold for us, but my own life history tells me that there will be days when I smile and days I cry—a mixture of days.

As I stood before the crowd, I reminded them about the tornados that came through our small town and completely wiped out an entire neighborhood and other places. During that time, I stood with a lady in her living room, where nothing remained except for the foundation. We stood there, and she told me where everything had been—as I looked at a concrete floor that was almost to the point of what it would have looked like in the building process many years before. I realized as I looked around and saw foundation after foundation how a foundation can withstand almost anything—and toilets, but that's neither here nor there.

In the book of Luke, Jesus talked about digging down deep and laying a foundation on the rock—a rock that we know is him. We have dug deep; I pray we have laid a foundation on Jesus that, when the floods of life come, won't allow the house to shake because it has been well built (Luke 6:48). As I have sought to build a foundation for my own life, I recognize what a privilege it has been to be able to share my journey with you. It is one I pray causes you to dig deep and build on Jesus!

As I finished sharing at the basketball game, some were smiling at me, one had tears welling up, and some looked bored stiff. I figure those of you reading this will have much the same reaction. Maybe if you make it this far, you're smiling. I wanted to apologize to the ones who looked uninterested and ask them not to judge Jesus if I had failed to hold their attention. I'm hoping you do the same.

After the game, I spoke with some of the people as they walked out. One or two hugged my neck. They made me smile big. Some nodded, and I smiled back. To those who got close enough where I could talk to them, I said the same thing I'm going to say to you:

Thank you for letting me share my heart with you. I pray yours is encouraged also.

Question to think about:

Share your testimony with the group.

Status Quo Challenge: Who will you share your testimony with this week?

Resources

I'm going to share a couple of resources which have helped me become focused more intently on my prayer life. One would be the book titled, "The Divine Hours", by Phyllis Tickle. There are several different books corresponding with the seasons. I ordered the Christmas one as I was writing this book. Then just this week, I walked into the thrift store and there on the shelf was the one for summer. For a dollar! I was so happy. Another great help has been the prayer journal by Debbie Taylor Williams, called "Prayers of My Heart". I have used her journals for the last several years. You can order both from any of the numerous retailers online.

Compassion International has been a blessing in my life. The days I get a letter from Onesmus brings untold joy to my heart. We have been sponsoring with them for the last four years. A year or so ago he contracted malaria. When Compassion sent me an email telling me he had contracted it, I was thrilled to know he was already receiving medical attention as a part of my normal monthly contribution. I would encourage you to visit Compassion's website and see if God would want you to be a part of what they are doing.

The questions that were included at the beginning and ending of each chapter were supplied by Ed Reed. A great guy, who always manages to spark some conversations when we all are together, some of them have become etched in my memory. Both of us pray that the questions caused the same type of conversations in your lives. Nothing makes us realize what we believe than when we pull it apart, dissect it, and then walk out the door to live it. Those types of discussions always make me pray harder and follow Jesus closer.

Notes

1. The NIV Application Commentary John
2. The Expositor's Bible Commentary, Volume 9. Pg. 92
3. For more information on Compassion International:
   www.compassion.org
4. "Kalos" http://www.blueletterbible.org/lang/lexicon/lexicon.
   cfm?Strongs=G2570&t=ESV
5. The NIV Application Commentary on John
6. http://www.amazon.com/Divine-Hours-Prayers-Autumn-
   Wintertime/dp/038550540X/ref=sr_1_6?s=books&ie=UTF
   8&qid=1327278545&sr=1-6
7. http://bible.org/seriespage/lame-excuse-preaching-gospel-
   acts-31-26
8. http://www.blueletterbible.org/lang/lexicon/lexicon.
   cfm?Strongs=G5485&t=ESV
9. http://www.blueletterbible.org/lang/lexicon/lexicon.
   cfm?Strongs=G5206&t=NIV
10. http://www.desiringgod.org/resource-library/sermons/i-am-
    who-i-am

More about Jenny

Jenny Smith is a wife to Chad and mom to three darling young women: Meghan, Katie, and Lauren. She teaches at her local church, conferences, retreats, banquets or wherever women gather to hear hope from God's Word for their lives. She is a graduate of She Speaks and can often be found surrounded by books, pen in hand, writing in her favorite notebook. She loves country life in Adairsville, Georgia. A country life that if her husband gets his wish will include chickens by the time you read this.

WEBSITE: If you enjoyed this book by Jenny, she would love to hear from you! You can find her website at www.keepinginstride.com. You'll also find additional resources available.

You can also send her an email at Jenny@keepinginstride.com or you'll find her frequently on FaceBook over at the Keeping In Stride page.

CPSIA information can be obtained at www.ICGtesting.com
Printed in the USA
LVOW040324290212

270852LV00001B/3/P